Globalization

Other Books in the Current Controversies Series

Globalization

Yea Jee Bae, Book Editor

GREENHAVEN
PUBLISHING

Published in 2019 by Greenhaven Publishing, LLC
353 3rd Avenue, Suite 255, New York, NY 10010

Copyright © 2019 by Greenhaven Publishing, LLC

First Edition

Articles in Greenhaven Publishing anthologies are often edited for length to meet page
requirements. In addition, original titles of these works are changed to clearly present
the main thesis and to explicitly indicate the author's opinion. Every effort is made to
ensure that Greenhaven Publishing accurately reflects the original intent of the authors.
Every effort has been made to trace the owners of the copyrighted material.

Cover image: Toria/Shutterstock.com

Library of Congress Cataloging-in-Publication Data

Names: Bae, Yea Jee, editor.
Title: Globalization / Yea Jee Bae, book editor.
Description: New York : Greenhaven Publishing, [2019] | Series: Current
  controversies | Audience: Grades 9 to 12. | Includes bibliographical
  references and index.
Identifiers: LCCN 2018029817| ISBN 9781534503861 (library bound) | ISBN
  9781534504592 (pbk.)
Subjects: LCSH: Globalization—Juvenile literature. | International economic
  relations—Juvenile literature. | Globalization—Social aspects—Juvenile
  literature.
Classification: LCC HF1365 .G5575 2018 | DDC 303.48/2—dc23
LC record available at https://lccn.loc.gov/2018029817

Manufactured in the United States of America

Website: http://greenhavenpublishing.com

Contents

Chapter 4: Does Economic Globalization Contribute to Poverty?

Baylee Molloy

Although it is difficult to make a definitive ruling on whether there is a causal relationship between globalization and poverty, there is research indicating significant changes in poverty levels in poor countries that are becoming integrated into the global economy.

Yes: Economic Globalization Increases Inequality

Anthony Amoah

In theory, free trade has great potential for increasing prosperity among nations. However, while international trade has aided the economic elite in developing countries, at the same time, it has exploited the poor labor force.

Nikil Savil

Public opinion toward globalization is changing as concerns about wage cuts and job losses increase. Evidence for worsening inequality implies that policymakers in business and finance are at least partially responsible.

No: Economic Globalization Helps the Poor

Jan Cienski

Although there is still a great number of poor people in the world, proportionally, the amount of the world's population living in poverty is lower than ever before. This is due to closer economic relationships between countries, reduced tariffs, and the increased flow of investments.

Foreword

"C ontroversy" is a word that has an undeniably unpleasant connotation. It carries a definite negative charge. Controversy can spoil family gatherings, spread a chill around classroom and campus discussion, inflame public discourse, open raw civic wounds, and lead to the ouster of public officials. We often feel that controversy is almost akin to bad manners, a rude and shocking eruption of that which must not be spoken or thought of in polite, tightly guarded society. To avoid controversy, to quell controversy, is often seen as a public good, a victory for etiquette, perhaps even a moral or ethical imperative.

Yet the studious, deliberate avoidance of controversy is also a whitewashing, a denial, a death threat to democracy. It is a false sterilizing, sanitizing, and superficial ordering of the messy, ragged, chaotic, at times ugly processes by which a healthy democracy identifies and confronts challenges, engages in passionate debate about appropriate approaches and solutions, and arrives at something like a consensus and a broadly accepted and supported way forward. Controversy is the megaphone, the speaker's corner, the public square through which the citizenry finds and uses its voice. Controversy is the life's blood of our democracy and absolutely essential to the vibrant health of our society.

Our present age is certainly no stranger to controversy. We are consumed by fierce debates about technology, privacy, political correctness, poverty, violence, crime and policing, guns, immigration, civil and human rights, terrorism, militarism, environmental protection, and gender and racial equality. Loudly competing voices are raised every day, shouting opposing opinions, putting forth competing agendas, and summoning starkly different visions of a utopian or dystopian future. Often these voices attempt to shout the others down; there is precious little listening and considering among the cacophonous din. Yet listening and considering, too, are essential to the health of a democracy. If controversy is democracy's lusty lifeblood, respectful listening and careful thought are its higher faculties, its brain, its conscience.

Current Controversies does not shy away from or attempt to hush the loudly competing voices. It seeks to provide readers with as wide and representative as possible a range of articulate voices on any given controversy of the day, separates each one out to allow it to be heard clearly and fairly, and encourages careful listening to each of these well-crafted, thoughtfully expressed opinions, supplied by some of today's leading academics, thinkers, analysts, politicians, policy makers, economists, activists, change agents, and advocates. Only after listening to a wide range of opinions on an issue, evaluating the strengths and weaknesses of each argument, assessing how well the facts and available evidence mesh with the stated opinions and conclusions, and thoughtfully and critically examining one's own beliefs and conscience can the reader begin to arrive at his or her own conclusions and articulate his or her own stance on the spotlighted controversy.

This process is facilitated and supported in each Current Controversies volume by an introduction and chapter overviews that provide readers with the essential context they need to begin engaging with the spotlighted controversies, with the debates surrounding them, and with their own perhaps shifting or nascent opinions on them. Chapters are organized around several key questions that are answered with diverse opinions representing all points on the political spectrum. In its content, organization, and methodology, readers are encouraged to determine the authors' point of view and purpose, interrogate and analyze the various arguments and their rhetoric and structure, evaluate the arguments' strengths and weaknesses, test their claims against available facts and evidence, judge the validity of the reasoning, and bring into clearer, sharper focus the reader's own beliefs and conclusions and how they may differ from or align with those in the collection or those of classmates.

Research has shown that reading comprehension skills improve dramatically when students are provided with compelling, intriguing, and relevant "discussable" texts. The subject matter of these collections could not be more compelling, intriguing, or urgently relevant to today's students and the world they are poised to inherit. The anthologized articles also provide the basis for stimulating, lively, and passionate classroom debates. Students who are compelled to anticipate objections to their own argument and identify the flaws in those of an opponent read more carefully, think more critically, and steep themselves in relevant context, facts, and information more thoroughly. In short, using discussable text of the kind provided by every single volume in the Current Controversies series encourages close reading, facilitates reading comprehension, fosters research, strengthens critical thinking, and greatly enlivens and energizes classroom discussion and participation. The entire learning process is deepened, extended, and strengthened.

If we are to foster a knowledgeable, responsible, active, and engaged citizenry, we must provide readers with the intellectual, interpretive, and critical-thinking tools and experience necessary to make sense of the world around them and of the all-important debates and arguments that inform it. We must encourage them not to run away from or attempt to quell controversy but to embrace it in a responsible, conscientious, and thoughtful way, to sharpen and strengthen their own informed opinions by listening to and critically analyzing those of others. This series encourages respectful engagement with and analysis of current controversies and competing opinions and fosters a resulting increase in the strength and rigor of one's own opinions and stances. As such, it helps readers assume their rightful place in the public square and provides them with the skills necessary to uphold their awesome responsibility—guaranteeing the continued and future health of a vital, vibrant, and free democracy.

Introduction

> *"No generation has had the opportunity, as we now have, to build a global economy that leaves no-one behind. It is a wonderful opportunity, but also a profound responsibility."*
>
> *—Former President Bill Clinton*

Globalization is a multifaceted concept that can be described in many ways depending on the context. In its simplest form, it is the movement of ideas, goods, and people between countries on a global scale. This may sound like a remote and abstract phenomenon, but its effects have already visibly permeated our daily lives. Imported goods, foreign films, the availability of local cuisines from around the world, and companies with branches overseas—these are all common examples of globalization at work. Driven by technological advancements and the removal of barriers to free trade, globalization has opened borders between nations, increasing the exchange of products and labor and creating an intermingling of cultural spheres. Whether these effects are for the better, however, is fiercely debated. Those in favor of globalization state that worldwide integration encourages economic growth and aids in the prosperity of all countries, while those in opposition criticize it for exploiting developing countries and not distributing its benefits equally across nations.

Although it has become a hot topic of late, globalization is not a new idea. It has been in practice for thousands of years—from the ancient trade network of the Silk Road to the work of early explorers like Vasco da Gama and Christopher Columbus in establishing new opportunities for commerce—and the term itself has been in mainstream usage since economist Theodore Levitt popularized it in his 1983 article, "The Globalization of Markets."[1] The difference in the present is that the trade and financial markets of today are much more advanced and widespread. In the twentieth century, there was an explosion of economic growth at a rapid rate incomparable to past growth trends. As developments in technology ushered in improvements to transportation and communication, the volume and range of trade was able to increase exponentially. Modern globalization takes place on an immensely larger geographical and economical scale than ever before. It could be said that the more the world expands, the closer it becomes.

A global market encourages competition and specialization, leading to greater business opportunities. People and businesses can efficiently specialize their goods and services according to their best skills and resources and access cheaper imports and increased exports. This type of international exchange can be of great benefit to nations that are without certain industries, like steel, or desired natural resources, like oil. If a country lacks the domestic ability to manufacture a product, it can still procure what it needs through trade. This gives consumers increased access to more goods at a competitive price, and such affordability can improve their standard of living.

Furthermore, an international exchange of information and technology allows for quicker economic progress and growth in less developed countries and more opportunities in open markets. The spread of electronic communication and increased access to the Internet has enabled people from all over the globe to become informed on what is going on in the world, procure shared knowledge, and become connected to one another. It fosters cooperation and a sense of mutual responsibility between countries, as evidenced by the creation of trade regulatory groups such as the International Monetary Fund in 1945 and the World Trade Organization in 1995.

At the same time, a prevalent concern is that a global economy encourages companies to capitalize on cheap labor in developing countries. Outsourcing overseas can allow multinational companies to exploit labor laws and low standards for increased profit margins, which often translates to poor working conditions and meager wages for their overseas workers. Simultaneously, this can diminish jobs and wages for workers at home, especially for those in less skilled occupations who may have difficulties transitioning to a new area of work. The spread of trade across the world also leaves behind an environmental footprint as manufacturing and transportation adds to pollution, and worldwide demand for products can lead to the overconsumption of resources.

Another fear of globalization is that social exchange may lead to a country's culture losing its unique qualities in favor of adopting a more globally homogenous outlook. This is particularly a concern with Western ideals; when presented by powerful, developed countries, these values have the potential to overtake local culture in an unbalanced exchange of culture and ideas. Globalization also raises ethical questions, as the wealth gained from this practice is not equally distributed to all the countries involved. The global average of per capita GDP has risen during the twentieth century, but with the richest quarter of the world experiencing an increase of nearly six-fold compared to the poorest quarter's less than three-fold, the distribution of wealth among countries has become more unequal than at the start of the century.[2]

With so many factors to consider, globalization is a complex topic requiring careful analysis, and one can easily become overwhelmed trying to sift through the prolific amount of available literature. *Current Controversies: Globalization* makes this process easier by providing a well-balanced variety of viewpoints on the subject without taking a side, giving readers the strong foundation necessary to start forming their own perspectives.

Notes

[1] "Theodore Levitt," The Economist, May 17, 2018. https://www.economist.com/node/13167376

[2] "Globalization: Threat or Opportunity?" International Monetary Fund, May 17, 2018. http://www.imf.org/external/np/exr/ib/2000/041200to.htm

CHAPTER 1

Are Countries Improved by Globalization?

The Complexities of Globalization Have Nuanced Effects

Lumen Learning

Lumen Learning uses open educational resources (OER) to craft low-cost course materials to replace cost-prohibitive textbooks. By applying science insights and learning data analysis to its materials, Lumen Learning's goal is to enable affordable and effective learning for all students.

Globalization refers to the process of integrating governments, cultures, and financial markets through international trade into a single world market. Often, the process begins with a single motive, such as market expansion (on the part of a corporation) or increased access to healthcare (on the part of a nonprofit organization). But usually there is a snowball effect, and globalization becomes a mixed bag of economic, philanthropic, entrepreneurial, and cultural efforts. Sometimes the efforts have obvious benefits, even for those who worry about cultural colonialism, such as campaigns to bring clean-water technology to rural areas that do not have access to safe drinking water.

Other globalization efforts, however, are more complex. Let us look, for example, at the North American Free Trade Agreement (NAFTA). The agreement is among the countries of North America, including Canada, the United States, and Mexico and allows much freer trade opportunities without the kind of tariffs (taxes) and import laws that restrict international trade. Often, trade opportunities are misrepresented by politicians and economists, who sometimes offer them up as a panacea to economic woes. For example, trade can lead to both increases and decreases in job opportunities. This is because while easier, more lax export laws mean there is the potential for job growth in the United States, imports can mean the exact opposite. As the United States import more goods from outside the country, jobs typically decrease, as more and more products are made overseas.

Many prominent economists believed that when NAFTA was created in 1994 it would lead to major gains in jobs. But by 2010, the evidence showed an opposite impact; the data showed 682,900 US jobs lost across all states (Parks 2011). While NAFTA did increase the flow of goods and capital across the northern and southern US borders, it also increased unemployment in Mexico, which spurred greater amounts of illegal immigration motivated by a search for work.

There are several forces driving globalization, including the global economy and multinational corporations that control assets, sales, production, and employment (United Nations 1973). Characteristics of multinational corporations include the following: A large share of their capital is collected from a variety of different nations, their business is conducted without regard to national borders, they concentrate wealth in the hands of core nations and already wealthy individuals, and they play a key role in the global economy.

We see the emergence of global assembly lines, where products are assembled over the course of several international transactions. For instance, Apple designs its next-generation Mac prototype in the United States, components are made in various peripheral nations, they are then shipped to another peripheral nation such as Malaysia for assembly, and tech support is outsourced to India.

Globalization has also led to the development of global commodity chains, where internationally integrated economic links connect workers and corporations for the purpose of manufacture and marketing (Plahe 2005). For example, in *maquiladoras*, mostly found in northern Mexico, workers may sew imported precut pieces of fabric into garments.

Globalization also brings an international division of labor, in which comparatively wealthy workers from core nations compete with the low-wage labor pool of peripheral and semi-peripheral nations. This can lead to a sense of xenophobia, which is an illogical fear and even hatred of foreigners and foreign goods. Corporations trying to maximize their profits in the United States are conscious of this risk and attempt to "Americanize" their products, selling shirts printed with US flags that were nevertheless made in Mexico.

Aspects of Globalization

Globalized trade is nothing new. Societies in ancient Greece and Rome traded with other societies in Africa, the Middle East, India, and China. Trade expanded further during the Islamic Golden Age and after the rise of the Mongol Empire. The establishment of colonial empires after the voyages of discovery by European countries meant that trade was going on all over the world. In the nineteenth century, the Industrial Revolution led to even more trade of ever-increasing amounts of goods. However, the advance of technology, especially communications, after World War II and the Cold War triggered the explosive acceleration in the process occurring today.

One way to look at the similarities and differences that exist among the economies of different nations is to compare their standards of living. The statistic most commonly used to do this is the domestic process per capita. This is the gross domestic product, or GDP, of a country divided by its population.

There are benefits and drawbacks to globalization. Some of the benefits include the exponentially accelerated progress of development, the creation of international awareness and empowerment, and the potential for increased wealth (Abedian 2002). However, experience has shown that countries can also be weakened by globalization. Some critics of globalization worry about the growing influence of enormous international financial and industrial corporations that benefit the most from free trade and unrestricted markets. They fear these corporations can use their vast wealth and resources to control governments to act in their interest rather than that of the local population (Bakan

2004). Indeed, when looking at the countries at the bottom of the list above, we are looking at places where the primary benefactors of mineral exploitation are major corporations and a few key political figures.

Other critics oppose globalization for what they see as negative impacts on the environment and local economies. Rapid industrialization, often a key component of globalization, can lead to widespread economic damage due to the lack of regulatory environment (Speth 2003). Further, as there are often no social institutions in place to protect workers in countries where jobs are scarce, some critics state that globalization leads to weak labor movements (Boswell and Stevis 1997). Finally, critics are concerned that wealthy countries can force economically weaker nations to open their markets while protecting their own local products from competition (Wallerstein 1974). This can be particularly true of agricultural products, which are often one of the main exports of poor and developing countries (Koroma 2007). In a 2007 article for the United Nations, Koroma discusses the difficulties faced by "least developed countries" (LDCs) that seek to participate in globalization efforts. These countries typically lack the infrastructure to be flexible and nimble in their production and trade, and therefore are vulnerable to everything from unfavorable weather conditions to international price volatility. In short, rather than offering them more opportunities, the increased competition and fast pace of a globalized market can make it more challenging than ever for LDCs to move forward (Koroma 2007).

The increasing use of outsourcing of manufacturing and service-industry jobs to developing countries has caused increased unemployment in some developed countries. Countries that do not develop new jobs to replace those that move, and train their labor force to do them, will find support for globalization weakening.

Summary

Globalization refers to the process of integrating governments, cultures, and financial markets through international trade into a single world market. There are benefits and drawbacks to globalization. Often the countries that fare the worst are those that depend on natural resource extraction for their wealth. Many critics fear globalization gives too much power to multinational corporations and that political decisions are influenced by these major financial players.

Globalization Spreads Freedom and Democracy

Daniel Griswold

Daniel Griswold is former director of the Cato Institute's Center for Trade Policy Studies and author of Mad about Trade: Why Main Street America Should Embrace Globalization.

When trade and globalization are discussed in the US Congress and in the American media, the focus is almost entirely on the economic impact at home—on manufacturing, jobs, and wages. But trade is about more than exporting soybeans and machine tools. It is also about exporting freedom and democracy.

Since September 11, 2001, the Bush administration has articulated the argument that trade can and must play a role in promoting democracy and human rights in the rest of the world. In an April 2002 speech, President Bush said, "Trade creates the habits of freedom," and those habits "begin to create the expectations of democracy and demands for better democratic institutions. Societies that are open to commerce across their borders are more open to democracy within their borders."

Trade, Development, and Political Reform

The connection between trade, development, and political reform is not just a throwaway line. In theory and in practice, economic and political freedoms reinforce one another. Political philosophers from Aristotle to Samuel Huntington have noted that economic development and an expanding middle class can provide more fertile ground for democracy.

Trade and globalization can spur political reform by expanding the freedom of people to exercise greater control over their daily

"Globalization, Human Rights, and Democracy," by Daniel Griswold, The Cato Institute, August 11, 2006. Reprinted by permission.

lives. In less developed countries, the expansion of markets means they no longer need to bribe or beg government officials for permission to import a television set or spare parts for their tractor. Controls on foreign exchange no longer limit their freedom to travel abroad. They can more easily acquire tools of communication such as mobile phones, Internet access, satellite TV, and fax machines.

As workers and producers, people in more open countries are less dependent on the authorities for their livelihoods. For example, in a more open, market-driven economy, the government can no longer deprive independent newspapers of newsprint if they should displease the ruling authorities. In a more open economy and society, the "CNN effect" of global media and consumer attention exposes and discourages the abuse of workers. Multinational companies have even greater incentives to offer competitive benefits and wages in more globalized developing countries than in those that are closed.

Economic freedom and rising incomes, in turn, help to nurture a more educated and politically aware middle class. A rising business class and wealthier civil society create leaders and centers of influence outside government. People who are economically free over time want and expect to exercise their political and civil rights as well. In contrast, a government that can seal its citizens off from the rest of the world can more easily control them and deprive them of the resources and information they could use to challenge its authority.

Increased Democratization

As theory would predict, trade, development, and political and civil freedom appear to be tied together in the real world. Everyone can agree that the world is more globalized than it was 30 years ago, but less widely appreciated is the fact that the world is much more democratized than it was 30 years ago. According to the most recent survey by Freedom House, the share of the world's population enjoying full political and civil freedoms has increased substantially in the past three decades, as has the share of the world's governments that are democratic.

In its annual survey, released in December 2005, the human rights research organization reported that 46 percent of the world's population now lives in countries it classifies as "Free," where citizens "enjoy open political competition, a climate of respect for civil liberties, significant independent civic life, and independent media." That compares to the 35 percent of mankind that enjoyed a similar level of freedom in 1973. The percentage of people in countries that are "Not Free," where political and civil liberties are systematically oppressed, dropped during the same period from 47 percent to 36 percent. The percentage of the population in countries that are "Partly Free" has remained at 18 percent. Meanwhile, the percentage of the world's governments that are democracies has reached 64 percent, the highest in the 33 years of Freedom House surveys.

Thanks in good measure to the liberating winds of globalization, the shift of 11 percentage points of the world's population in the past three decades from "Not Free" to "Free" means that another 650 million human beings today enjoy the kind of civil and political liberties taken for granted in such countries as the United States, Japan, and Belgium, instead of suffering under the kind of tyranny we still see in the most repressive countries.

Within individual countries, economic and political freedoms also appear to be linked. A 2004 study by the Cato Institute, titled "Trading Tyranny for Freedom," found that countries that are relatively open to the global economy are much more likely to be democracies that respect civil and political liberties than those that are relatively closed. And relatively closed countries are far more likely to deny systematically civil and political liberties than those that are open.

From Economic Reform to Political Reform

In the past two decades, a number of economies have followed the path of economic and trade reform leading to political reform.

South Korea and Taiwan as recently as the 1980s were governed by authoritarian regimes that did not permit much open dissent. Today, after years of expanding trade and rising incomes, both are multiparty democracies with full political and civil liberties. Other countries that have most aggressively followed those twin tracks of reform include Chile, Ghana, Hungary, Mexico, Nicaragua, Paraguay, Portugal, and Tanzania.

In other words, governments that grant their citizens a large measure of freedom to engage in international commerce find it increasingly difficult to deprive them of political and civil liberties, while governments that "protect" their citizens behind tariff walls and other barriers to international commerce find it much easier to deny those same liberties. Of course, the correlation between economic openness and political freedom across countries is not perfect, but the broad trends are undeniable.

The application for US foreign policy is that trade and development, along with its economic benefits, can prove to be powerful tools for spreading broader freedoms and democracy around the world.

In mainland China, for example, economic reform and globalization give reason to hope for political reforms. After 25 years of reform and rapid growth, an expanding middle class is experiencing for the first time the independence of home ownership, travel abroad, and cooperation with others in economic enterprise free of government control. The number of telephone lines, mobile phones, and Internet users has risen exponentially in the past decade. Millions of Chinese students and tourists travel abroad each year. That can only be good news for individual freedom in China, and a growing problem for the government.

Free trade and globalization can also play a role in promoting democracy and human rights in the Middle East. In a May 2003 address outlining his plan for a Middle East free trade area, President Bush said, "The Arab world has a great cultural tradition, but is largely missing out on the economic progress of our time.

Across the globe, free markets and trade have helped defeat poverty, and taught men and women the habits of liberty."

Economic stagnation in the Middle East feeds terrorism, not because of poverty but because of a lack of opportunity and hope for a better future, especially among the young. Young people who cannot find meaningful work and who cannot participate in the political process are ripe pickings for religious fanatics and terrorist recruiters. Any effort to encourage greater freedom in the Middle East must include an agenda for promoting economic liberty and openness.

The Future

On a multilateral level, a successful agreement through the World Trade Organization (WTO) would create a more friendly climate globally for democracy and human rights. Less developed countries, by opening up their own, relatively closed markets and gaining greater access to rich-country markets, could achieve higher rates of growth and develop the expanding middle class that forms the backbone of most democracies. A successful conclusion of the WTO Doha Development Round of trade negotiations that began in 2001 would reinforce the twin trends of globalization and the spread of political and civil liberties that have marked the last 30 years. Failure would delay and frustrate progress on both fronts for millions of people.

For the past three decades, globalization, human rights, and democracy have been marching forward together, haltingly, not always and everywhere in step, but in a way that unmistakably shows they are interconnected. By encouraging globalization in less developed countries, we not only help to raise growth rates and incomes, promote higher standards, and feed, clothe, and house the poor; we also spread political and civil freedoms.

Trade Raises Incomes, Stimulates Economic Growth, and Encourages Good Government

World Trade Organization

The World Trade Organization (WTO) is an international governmental organization that regulates trade between nations. A large majority of the world's trading nations have negotiated, signed, and ratified the WTO's agreements, laying the legal ground rules for international commerce.

The world is complex. This booklet is brief, but it tries to reflect the complex and dynamic nature of trade. It highlights some of the benefits of the WTO's "trading system," but it doesn't claim that everything is perfect—otherwise there would be no need for further negotiations and for the system to evolve and reform continually.

Nor does it claim that everyone agrees with everything in the WTO. That's one of the most important reasons for having the system: it's a forum for countries to thrash out their differences on trade issues.

That said, there are many over-riding reasons why we're better off with the system than without it. Here are 10 of them.

[...]

The System Helps to Keep the Peace

Peace is partly an outcome of two of the most fundamental principles of the trading system: helping trade to flow smoothly, and providing countries with a constructive and fair outlet for dealing with disputes over trade issues. It is also an outcome of the international confidence and cooperation that the system creates and reinforces.

History is littered with examples of trade disputes turning into war. One of the most vivid is the trade war of the 1930s

"10 Benefits of the WTO Trading System," World Trade Organization, July 2007. Reprinted by permission.

when countries competed to raise trade barriers in order to protect domestic producers and retaliate against each others' barriers. This worsened the Great Depression and eventually played a part in the outbreak of World War II.

Two developments immediately after the Second World War helped to avoid a repeat of the pre-war trade tensions. In Europe, international cooperation developed in coal, and in iron and steel. Globally, the General Agreement on Tariffs and Trade (GATT) was created.

Both have proved successful, so much so that they are now considerably expanded—one has become the European Union, the other the World Trade Organization (WTO).

How Does This Work?

Crudely put, sales people are usually reluctant to fight their customers. In other words, if trade flows smoothly and both sides enjoy a healthy commercial relationship, political conflict is less likely.

What's more, smoothly-flowing trade also helps people all over the world become better off. People who are more prosperous and contented are also less likely to fight.

[...]

The System Allows Disputes to Be Handled Constructively

There could be a down side to trade liberalization and expansion. More trade means more opportunities for disputes to arise. Left to themselves, those disputes could lead to serious conflict. But in reality, a lot of international trade tension is reduced because countries can turn to organizations, in particular the WTO, to settle their trade disputes.

Before World War II that option was not available. After the war, the world's community of trading nations negotiated trade rules which are now entrusted to the WTO. Those rules include an obligation for members to bring their disputes to the WTO and not to act unilaterally.

When they bring disputes to the WTO, the WTO's procedure focuses their attention on the rules. Once a ruling has been made, countries concentrate on trying to comply with the rules, and perhaps later renegotiating the rules—not on declaring war on each other.

Around 300 disputes have been brought to the WTO since it was set up in 1995. Without a means of tackling these constructively and harmoniously, some could have led to more serious political conflict.

[…]

A System Based on Rules Rather than Power Makes Life Easier for All

Decisions in the WTO are made by consensus. The WTO agreements were negotiated by all members, were approved by consensus and were ratified in all members' parliaments. The agreements apply to everyone. Rich and poor countries alike have an equal right to challenge each other in the WTO's dispute settlement procedures.

This makes life easier for all, in several different ways. Smaller countries can enjoy some increased bargaining power. Without a multilateral regime such as the WTO's system, the more powerful countries would be freer to impose their will unilaterally on their smaller trading partners. Smaller countries would have to deal with each of the major economic powers individually, and would be much less able to resist unwanted pressure.

[…]

There are matching benefits for larger countries. The major economic powers can use the single forum of the WTO to negotiate with all or most of their trading partners at the same time. This makes life much simpler for the bigger trading countries. The alternative would be continuous and complicated bilateral negotiations with dozens of countries simultaneously. And each country could end up with different conditions for trading with each of its trading partners, making life extremely complicated for its importers and exporters.

[…]

Freer Trade Cuts the Cost of Living

Protectionism is expensive: it raises prices. The WTO's global system lowers trade barriers through negotiation and applies the principle of non-discrimination. The result is reduced costs of production (because imports used in production are cheaper) and reduced prices of finished goods and services, and ultimately a lower cost of living.

[…]

It Gives Consumers More Choice, and a Broader Range of Qualities to Choose From

Think also of the things people in other countries can have because they buy exports from us and elsewhere. Look around and consider all the things that would disappear if all our imports were taken away from us. Imports allow us more choice—both more goods and services to choose from, and a wider range of qualities. Even the quality of locally-produced goods can improve because of the competition from imports.

The wider choice isn't simply a question of consumers buying foreign finished products. Imports are used as materials, components and equipment for local production.

This expands the range of final products and services that are made by domestic producers, and it increases the range of technologies they can use. When mobile telephone equipment became available, services sprang up even in the countries that did not make the equipment, for example.

[…]

Trade Raises Incomes

The WTO's own estimates for the impact of the 1994 Uruguay Round trade deal were between $109 billion and $510 billion added to world income (depending on the assumptions of the calculations and allowing for margins of error).

More recent research has produced similar figures. Economists estimate that cutting trade barriers in agriculture, manufacturing and services by one third would boost the world economy by $613 billion—equivalent to adding an economy the size of Canada to the world economy.

[...]

So trade clearly boosts incomes. Trade also poses challenges as domestic producers face competition from imports. But the fact that there is additional income means that resources are available for governments to redistribute the benefits from those who gain the most—for example to help companies and workers adapt by becoming more productive and competitive in what they were already doing, or by switching to new activities.

Trade Stimulates Economic Growth, and That Can Be Good News for Employment

This is a difficult subject to tackle in simple terms. There is strong evidence that trade boosts economic growth, and that economic growth means more jobs. It is also true that some jobs are lost even when trade is expanding. But a reliable analysis of this poses at least two problems.

First, there are other factors at play. For example, technological advance has also had a strong impact on employment and productivity, benefiting some jobs, hurting others.

Second, while trade clearly boosts national income (and prosperity), this is not always translated into new employment for workers who lost their jobs as a result of competition from imports.

[...]

The Basic Principles Make the System Economically More Efficient, and They Cut Costs

Trade allows a division of labour between countries. It allows resources to be used more appropriately and effectively for production. But the WTO's trading system offers more than that. It helps to increase efficiency and to cut costs even more because of important principles enshrined in the system.

Imagine a situation where each country sets different rules and different customs duty rates for imports coming from different trading partners. Imagine that a company in one country wants to import raw materials or components—copper for wiring or printed circuit boards for electrical goods, for example—for its own production.

[...]

A System Shields Governments from Narrow Interests

One of the lessons of the protectionism that dominated the early decades of the 20th century was the damage that can be caused if narrow sectoral interests gain an unbalanced share of political influence. The result was increasingly restrictive policy which turned into a trade war that no one won and everyone lost.

Superficially, restricting imports looks like an effective way of supporting an economic sector. But it biases the economy against other sectors which shouldn't be penalized—if you protect your clothing industry, everyone else has to pay for more expensive clothes, which puts pressure on wages in all sectors, for example.

Protectionism can also escalate as other countries retaliate by raising their own trade barriers. That's exactly what happened in the 1920s and 30s with disastrous effects. Even the sectors demanding protection ended up losing.

[...]

The System Encourages Good Government

The rules include commitments not to backslide into unwise policies. Protectionism in general is unwise because of the damage it causes domestically and internationally, as we have already seen.

Particular types of trade barriers cause additional damage because they provide opportunities for corruption and other forms of bad government.

One kind of trade barrier that the WTO's rules try to tackle is the quota, for example restricting imports or exports to no more than a specific amount each year.

Because quotas limit supply, they artificially raise prices, creating abnormally large profits (economists talk about "quota rent"). That profit can be used to influence policies because more money is available for lobbying.

[…]

Transparency (such as making available to the public all information on trade regulations), other aspects of "trade facilitation," clearer criteria for regulations dealing with the safety and standards of products, and nondiscrimination also help by reducing the scope for arbitrary decision-making and cheating.

[…]

Increased Offshoring Has Damaged the US Economy

Alex Lach

Alex Lach is a former political and nonprofit consultant who worked for the Center for American Progress. He is a graduate of Tufts University with a degree in political science.

The ongoing national debate about the employment practices of US companies and private equity firms abroad features two phrases that confuse rather than clarify the issues: offshoring and outsourcing. For most Americans, the phrases are interchangeable, referring to the agonizing loss of jobs here in the United States, many in manufacturing, to workers abroad—aided and abetted by US businesses and investors.

Indeed, a large percentage of Americans are concerned about jobs shifting from the United States to other countries. And they don't put much stock into whether those jobs stay within a particular company or are contracted to a third party when the ultimate outcome is jobs lost at home. This is why most Americans find debates about outsourcing versus offshoring to be meaningless. To them it is all about the overseas outsourcing of jobs.

Still, before we present the five most important facts about overseas outsourcing, let's first get the definitions right. According to Plunkett Research, a leading research group on outsourcing and offshoring practices, offshoring refers to:

> The tendency among many US, Japanese and Western European firms to send both knowledge-based and manufacturing work to third-party firms in other nations. Often, the intent is to take advantage of lower wages and operating costs.

This Material ("5 Facts About Overseas Outsourcing", by Alex Lach, Center for American Progress, July 9, 2012.) was created by the Center for American Progress (americanprogress.org). Reprinted by permission..

This differs from outsourcing, which Plunkett Research defines as "as the hiring of an outside company to perform a task that would otherwise be performed internally by a company." The difference lies in the fact that outsourcing can take place within our domestic borders or abroad. But for the purposes of this column we will examine the combination of outsourcing to other countries and offshoring, and refer to the combination of these practices as "overseas outsourcing."

So how pervasive is overseas outsourcing in our economy? Comprehensive data on overseas outsourcing practices are hard to establish, due in large part to limited government information which, according to the Congressional Research Service, were "not designed to link employment gains or losses in the United States, either for individual jobs, individual companies or in the aggregate, with the gains and losses of jobs abroad."

Furthermore, companies attempt to limit exposure of their overseas outsourcing practices, leading researchers to believe that even the most extensive methodologies only capture one-third of all production shifts. Still, there are important factors to understand about outsourcing as the debate makes its way back onto the national stage. Here are the top five trends:

US Multinationals Shifted Millions of Jobs Overseas in the 2000s

Data from the US Department of Commerce showed that "US multinational corporations, the big brand-name companies that employ a fifth of all American workers... cut their work forces in the US by 2.9 million during the 2000s while increasing employment overseas by 2.4 million."

Furthermore, a recent *Wall Street Journal* analysis showed, "Thirty-five big US-based multinational companies added jobs much faster than other US employers in the past two years, but nearly three-fourths of those jobs were overseas."

As Overseas Outsourcing Has Expanded, US Manufacturing Has Suffered the Brunt of the Blow

According to a report on outsourcing by Working America, "Manufacturing employment collapsed from a high of 19.5 million workers in June 1979 to 11.5 workers in December 2009, a drop of 8 million workers over 30 years. Between August 2000 and February 2004, manufacturing jobs were lost for a stunning 43 consecutive months—the longest such stretch since the Great Depression." Manufacturing plants have also declined sharply in the last decade, shrinking by more than 51,000 plants, or 12.5 percent, between 1998 and 2008. These stable, middle-class jobs have been the driving force of the US economy for decades and these losses have done considerable damage to communities across the country.

The Global Electronics Contract Manufacturing Industry Reached a Staggering $360 Billion of Revenue in 2011, and Is Expected to Expand to $426 Billion by 2015

This figure consists of companies, many of which are American, contracting outside firms largely in third-world countries with cheaper labor costs to manufacture their products. While this figure is not exclusively US companies, large corporations such as Apple Inc., which conducts all of its manufacturing on foreign shores, and Nike Inc., which subcontracts all of its footwear production to independently owned and operated foreign companies, lead the trend.

Private Equity Firms Have Increased the Pressure to Cut Costs By Any Means Necessary, Leading to More Overseas Outsourcing

Steve Pearlstein, a professor of public and international affairs at George Mason University and a Pulitzer-prize winning columnist, details the overseas outsourcing done by private equity firms in the 1980s, beginning with:

A wave of corporate takeovers, many of them unwanted and uninvited. Corporate executives came to fear that if they did not run their businesses with the aim of maximizing short-term profits and share prices, their companies would become takeover targets and they would be out of a job. Overnight, outsourcing became a manhood test for corporate executives.

For the private equity firms that took over companies, "the standard strategy has been to load up company executives with so much stock and stock options that they don't hesitate to make difficult decisions such as shedding divisions, closing plants or outsourcing work overseas."

Labor Costs Are the Main Driver of Corporations Sending Jobs Overseas, but Foreign Countries' Costs Are Increasing Compared to the United States

According to a 2012 survey from Duke's Fuqua School of Business, nearly three-quarters of respondents indicated labor cost savings as one of the three most important drivers leading to overseas outsourcing. This was twice the rate of response for any other option. But according to research from the Hackett Group, the cost gap between the United States and China has shrunk by nearly 50 percent over the past eight years, and is expected to stand at just 16 percent by 2013. Labor costs in China and elsewhere are rising, and coupled with rising fuel prices raising shipping costs, the economic argument for sending jobs overseas may be becoming less persuasive.

Despite these increasing costs, the Duke survey found that "only 4 percent of large companies had future plans for relocating jobs back to the United States." The Duke survey does not identify the reasons for this reluctance to bring these jobs back to our country, but a key factor could be the US tax code, which, as Seth Hanlon explains, "rewards companies for making investments abroad—and leads to them shifting offices, factories, and jobs abroad even if similar investments in the United States would be more profitable absent tax considerations."

Industrial Pollution Has Dangerously Lowered Air Quality Worldwide

Hugh Roberts

Hugh Roberts is an international urban planner who has spent over forty years working on the master planning, design, and development of new towns and urban infrastructure.

The World Health Organisation (WHO) expect poor air quality worldwide to be the leading cause of premature deaths by 2050. They probably look back at the Paris Climate Accord of December 2015 with mixed emotions. First off, replicating the wide consensus about climate change for the effects of air pollution on population health would be a worthy ambition. Then again, they must now look at how recent populist resistance, particularly by the Trump presidency in the US, has set back the cause of legislating against environmental degradation. They might wish for no more horse-trading over whys and wherefores, just consensus on what needs to be done, then getting on with it.

But in seeking agreement on how to improve air quality, WHO do themselves few favors. Their standard parameter of suffering from poor health is the Disability Adjusted Life Year or "DALY," measuring numbers of years lost to ill health, disability or death, against a notional average healthy life expectancy. Not surprisingly, this peasoup of statistical complexity is argued over by medics, demographers and sociologists threatening the capacity to agree anything about how to tackle the poisoning of our lungs.

We all accept the root causes of poor air; most are man made. They include the vastly increased reliance on the internal combustion engine over the last half-century, particularly in rapidly growing economies. But emissions from industrial processes, and urbanisation with its encroachment on previous areas of virgin, or

"The Problem of Global Air Pollution," University of Oxford/Oxford Today, July 11, 2017. Reprinted by permission.

partly domesticated natural vegetation, are just as guilty. Nature adds its own contribution via volcanic emissions and the minority of forest fires not started by man, but largely we are responsible for the deteriorating quality of the air we breathe. We know the causes, so we should be able to identify the solutions to slow and eventually stop, worldwide decline in air quality.

In most developed economies, there are some promising starts. Coal-fired power generation is now a fraction of what it was 30 years ago. Sustainably sourced generation continues to rise as its lifetime and operating costs continue to fall. We still have a way to go on vehicle emissions, but again we've made a start. Old vehicle scrapping schemes, congestion charging and a new wave of road pricing all act to encourage more use of public transport and ultra low emission zones will soon make it too expensive to move freight with anything other than vehicles with the cleanest emissions, if not electric motivation. These measures cannot come soon enough for cities across the developed world where climate warming over the last two decades is exacerbating toxic air quality.

But how can we deliver such improvements to developing economies where the worst air quality deterioration is found? Not, I suggest, by arguing endlessly over the health statistics. We need positive and practical measures on the ground.

Schemes scrapping aging and inefficient cars for those with more efficient engines would have a major impact in fast developing economies, where reliance on private vehicles is the only solution for the livelihoods of marginally coping communities. A subsidy scheme by motor industry offenders over recent NOx emission cheating, replacing old with new models might be too much to hope for, but consumer loyalty would be engendered worldwide by an international gesture of this sort. VW and others, are you listening?

Greater investment in public transport infrastructure is at last becoming a viable sector for the finance industry, as it seeks out longer term returns for its insurance and pensions customers. Only the most secure covenants are attracting the right quality of project funding capital, but where this ventures into developing economies, it needs underwriting via World Bank and other overseas aid agencies.

Hydrocarbons-fired power generation in, for example China and South East Asia, as already in the west, needs steady replacement by sustainable sources, as already occurring in the west. Those losing jobs in mining and facing the burden of unemployment, could be re-trained to manufacturing jobs in fast-growing renewables. There is ample experience to build on here from across western Europe. Rapidly reducing costs of sustainable energy generation needs importing to economies where they will soon be needed most to compete with continued low labour costs in mining and extraction.

Finally, urban planning has to become a stronger feature of land use management, thus optimising development of previously green space on the edges of towns, and only allowing urbanisation to expand beyond current city limits where take-up of underused space inside the urban envelope is impossible. Effective land use management has a huge if indirect contribution to make to reduce air pollution.

The long-term effects of degraded air are measurable in the treatment of respiratory disorders and associated loss of earnings or death with its associated dependencies from what would otherwise be healthy populations. Society has to develop cross accounting, so that the costs of installing physical infrastructure now, pay for reduced health care later. Only by making such mould-breaking accounting solutions work effectively, will we achieve the benefits of a truly joined-up world economy.

CHAPTER 2

Are Multinational Corporations Unethical?

Corporate Interests Have Displaced Public and Governmental Authority

Share the World's Resources

Share the World's Resources (STWR) is an independent nonprofit civil society organization that campaigns for fairer sharing of wealth, power, and resources between countries.

The type of economic enterprise that concerns us in this analysis is the small number of corporations that exert an excessive influence over many aspects of global economic, political and social life. They operate in multiple countries, in all commercial markets and share similar business models, assumptions and structures. The vast majority of corporations are publicly traded and their shares are mainly owned by other corporations, senior board members, a few wealthy stake holders and, indirectly, the public through investment institutions such as insurance companies and pension funds.

These corporations thrive best in an economy where market forces determine the production, price and supply of goods and services. This fact is mirrored in the prevailing attitude to the economy that dominant governments, economists and industrialists maintain. The argument is that centrally planned economies are less efficient and are unresponsive to consumer demand. They argue that to achieve efficiency, government intervention needs to be reduced to a minimum and the democratic, public control of the economy minimized. Thus, free trade and neoliberal policies are being actively promoted through international bodies such as the WTO, World Bank and IMF.

However, this argument is flawed. For a start, corporations are themselves centrally planned economies. Decisions are not open

"Multinational Corporations (MNCs): Beyond The Profit Motive," Share the World's Resources, October 3, 2006. https://www.sharing.org/information-centre/reports/multinational-corporations-mncs-beyond-profit-motive. Licensed Under CC BY-NC-ND 2.0 UK.

to question within a corporation and absolute control is exercised over production and distribution networks by management. Also, whereas public companies are required to be transparent to public scrutiny, the contracts that corporations have with respect to resource management or service delivery remain a commercial secret, removing an important level of accountability.

Many of these unaccountable corporations now have a greater turnover than the GDP of most countries. Of the 100 largest economies in the world, 52 are corporations and 48 are countries, and these corporations have sales figures between $51 billion and $247 billion. Seventy percent of world trade is controlled by just 500 of the largest industrial corporations, and in 2002, the top 200 had combined sales equivalent to 28% of world GDP. However, these 200 corporations only employed 0.82% of the global work force, highlighting the reduction in employment created by excessive economies of scale. In the US, ninety-eight percent of all companies account for only 25 percent of business activity; the remaining two percent account for nearly 75 percent of the remaining activity. The top 500 industrial corporations, which represent only one-tenth of one percent of all US companies, control over two-thirds of the business resources in the US and collect over 70 percent of all US profits. Thus there is also a disproportionate distribution of financial benefit from economic activity, which clearly does not pass to local communities through opportunity or wages. It is retained instead by a small number of major shareholders of an even smaller number of corporations.

Whereas corporations are based mainly in affluent countries such as the US, the EU, Japan, Canada and Australia, their key markets, productive facilities and many of their resources are based in or extracted from developing countries. According to the International Finance Corporation (IFC), inflows of foreign direct investment to the emerging markets have grown by an average of 23 percent per year between 1990 and 2000. The combined value of stock markets in emerging economies is set to exceed $5 trillion in 2006, and has more than doubled in the past decade.

As corporations grow, they find it economically beneficial (profitable) to operate in multiple countries, seeking out favourable conditions such as low labour costs, fewer regulations and other financial or tax incentives. Many of these multinational corporations can now be described as 'transnational', as they have 'globalized' their operations and retain no particular affiliation to any country. This allows them greater flexibility in operative structure and greater leverage over governments who compete for their business.

The convergence of economic power has created a concentration of political influence in society which is reflected nationally and globally. The resulting influence of the private sector has manipulated global economic, political and public thinking and established an unsustainable, consumerist culture.

[...]

The History of Corruption

The Beginning

In 16th century Britain, the majority of corporations were charitable institutions licensed by the crown and forbidden to engage in profitable commercial activities. At the time the prevailing business model was that of partnerships of individuals who pooled their resources and acted in the interests of their own communities. Limited liability corporations were generally distrusted by most, including Adam Smith, and due to widespread corruption and fraud, they were at one stage banned for more than 50 years in the UK.

However, a few corporations were deemed to be acting directly in the nation's interest as they engaged in very large-scale, high-risk commercial activities. For example, the Massachusetts Bay Company was chartered by King Charles I in 1638 in order to colonize the new world, and it settled in the United States. This and similar companies, such as the Dutch East India Company and the British East India Company, were a crucial part of the mercantile economic policies practiced by the colonial powers who were effectively running state monopolies in their colonies. These corporations were able to accumulate great financial and economic power through publicly trading shares in their companies.

The US experience of corporate monopolies enforced upon them by their colonial rulers reinforced their dislike of the corporate structure. The public and the courts were acutely aware that corporate bodies could amass undue public wealth and have excessive control over resources, production, the media and the electoral process. As a result, these powers were considered unconstitutional and held in check. Corporations could not indulge in activities which their charter did not specify, and they could not hold stock in other corporations. Some states even banned private banking charters altogether. Legislators, not courts, would cautiously grant limited charters and would hold business owners liable for any harms or injuries to persons or the community. Corporate charters were not granted freely until the mid 19th century. Until then the preferred method of economic organization was unincorporated business associations, cooperatives and publicly funded social services such as universities, libraries and firehouses. Agriculture, manufacturing, municipal markets and warehouses were all promoted and subsidized locally.

This changed prior to the American Civil War, as corporations started to abuse their charters and amassed private fortunes by creating conglomerates and trusts. The advent of the Civil War further increased their wealth and power as they benefited from the massive government spending that usually accompanies military conflict. As they learned to use their economic and political wealth more effectively, modern corporations exerted more and more influence over democratic life in the US. They used their wealth and influence to bribe officials at all levels of government, and influence court decisions. In return, governments handed over public resources such as land, water, timber and minerals, and granted massive financial subsidies. Most worryingly, they began influencing governments and courts, which secured them constitutional rights that were, up until that point, designed to protect people and their civil liberties.

Securing Legal Rights

Corporate lawyers established the precedent of 'Corporate Personhood' in US law, which granted them the same constitutional rights as ordinary people. They first began manipulating the courts perception of the Fourteenth Amendment, originally designed to protect the civil rights of slaves. They argued that 'equal protection rights' and 'Due Process' should apply to corporations as well as people, and in 1889, the supreme court bestowed these rights on corporations under the authority of the Fourteenth Amendment. Thus corporations became 'persons'. This was a major turning point, allowing corporations to use these new powers to undermine the democratic rights that the constitution originally intended to confer on citizens: the right to a republican form of government, derived exclusively from the consent of the governed.

The enshrining of limited liability in British and US law in the latter half of the 19th century removed the risk factor from corporate business. It allowed investment funds to be obtained by the public trading of company shares, without imparting any legal responsibility upon the shareholders for the actions of the company. One by one, states in the US began encouraging local investment by lifting restrictions that prevented corporations from merging and acquiring other corporations and stock. Soon corporations were allowed to exist indefinitely and have business multiple interests in multiple states.

In 1906, corporate lawyers secured Fourth Amendment Constitutional Rights for their clients, which originally protected people's possessions from unreasonable searches. The corporations used this protection to limit health, safety and environmental investigations in corporate facilities and to keep corporate documents private. This has undermined the public's right to proper heath and safety standards and environmental protection ever since.

Corporations were also granted protection under the Fifth Amendment, preventing corporate powers from being revoked without due process. This allowed corporations to be compensated if they loose revenue from local laws designed to protect citizens.

Under the First Amendment (Freedom of Speech) corporations have been granted the right to influence legislation that is unrelated to their business. As a result corporations have infringed upon the very heart of democracy. States can no longer limit corporate advertising, even when politically motivated, or limit financial contributions to political campaigns.

These, and other changes, have undermined the people's right to treat corporations as subordinate, man-made entities. Corporate rights now directly compete with the public's right to their health, safety and welfare. The courts have chosen not to address this conflict of interest and the undermining of the democratic process. They have instead allowed modern corporations to use these rights to amass greater wealth. Economic power creates political influence, a fact that, given their new protections under US law, corporations use to their full advantage.

As the financial markets flourished in the early 20th century, the US continued on its prosperous path. The concept of private wealth generation soon dominated political and economic thought, and even the shift of emphasis to social concerns during the great depression of the 20's did little to change this view. Soon, the corporate agenda went global, spurred on by the US foreign policy objectives. A window of opportunity opened after the 2nd world war which allowed the US to create favourable trading conditions with a war torn Europe. Although generous assistance was provided through the Marshall Plan, the creation of the Bretton Woods institutions (IMF, World Bank and GATT) secured US dominance of international trade and finance, guaranteeing future US prosperity. The government's tools for global economic exploitation were their faithful corporations.

Dominating the Global Economy

More recently, corporations realized that it was possible to dramatically increase profits by shifting their operations to developing countries where wages, costs and taxes were much lower, and regulation almost nonexistent. This was achieved through the Bretton Woods Trio and free trade agreements.

The World Bank has proven to be profitable to large corporations based in the north, initiating large-scale development programs in poor countries that attract private investment. Foreign direct investment now exceeds $1 trillion per year for projects such as privatization of public utilities and creating banking systems—such projects are clearly safe bets for corporate investors. Again there is a stark concentration of political and economic power here, as 1% of all multinationals own 50% of the total stock of all foreign direct investment.

Whilst the World Bank inflates Third World borrowing for development projects, the IMF acts as the lender of last resort for the balance of payment deficits often experienced by developing countries. The combined result of these actions is massive indebtedness for impoverished countries. To guarantee returns, these same institutions impose structural adjustment programs on borrowing countries to prioritize debt repayment. This proved lucrative for financial corporations based in the north, whose interests the IMF has openly defended. When these corporations made bad loans to developing countries, the IMF provided multi billion dollar bailouts. For example, it bailed out foreign investors in Russia with an $11 billion package and orchestrated a massive bailout of the big banks that made bad loans to Asian countries. In 1995, the IMF gave almost $18 billion to Wall Street investors who stood to lose billions with the peso devaluation.

In 1995, the General Agreement on Tariffs and Trade (GATT) was replaced by the World Trade Organization (WTO), which has worked closely with corporations in world trade negotiations. The WTO membership confers upon its member countries absolute adherence to its regulations and agreements. The agreements specify that WTO trade rules supersede any domestic laws and regulations which arguably restrict trade in any way. In this way, environmental, safety and labour laws are regularly circumvented since they can potentially reduce commercial activity. As a result, the WTO is effectively the world's highest legislative body. WTO rulings have often resulted in national governments being sued by corporations simply for placing national interests above corporate profit. The overall effect is the harmonizing of international regulations and standards to their lowest denominator, an outcome that is welcomed by the multinationals.

[…]

Conclusion

The growth of corporate rights, economic power and political influence has mainly been confined to the past 150 years, although the seeds of corporate domination rest in more distant mercantilist and colonial practices. On the surface, the global political, economic and cultural landscape has changed dramatically over this period, and democracy is in its ascendancy. However, it is undeniable that over the same period of time, the people's democratic right to determine their economic life has been superseded by corporate interests. This consolidation of political power comes at the expense of public authority and continues to stimulate strong opposition globally. It is maintained by the neo-liberal policies being pursued on a global scale.

In line with historic conflicts all over the world, the current battle is between the global public and the corporate and political elite over the control of government. Who decides how people organize and live their lives? Who decides if people go with or without water, food, healthcare or education? These rights must rest with the global public and their representative bodies, and not with a tiny minority who directly benefit from an ideology that shrinks public involvement in these central decisions.

Corporations are not people. They do not exist without shareholders and they exist only for profit. They are incapable of demonstrating the same values that people hold and express within their communities. The US constitution was never meant to represent the rights of economic entities; there is no mention of corporations or other such entities in the constitution. The corporation must not enjoy the protection of the Bill of Rights. In a true democracy, corporations must exist at the pleasure of the people and under their sovereignty.

[…]

Multinational Corporations Create Dependency in Their Host Countries

Dan-Jumbo Comfort T. and Akpan Ekom Etim

Dan-Jumbo Comfort T. is affiliated with the department of hospitality management and tourism at the University of Port Harcourt in Nigeria. Akpan Ekom Etim is affiliated with the department of management at the University of Port Harcourt.

The growing importance of multinational corporations in the global economy, international trade policy formulation and implementation can no longer be ignored by scholars, management experts, consultants and corporations. This has brought increase attention on the perceived contributions of multinational corporations on economic development of nations. As noted by Kumar (2015) in the current competitive level of the global economy, multinational corporations play an indispensable role especially in an emerging economy like Nigeria.

In a recent study, Osuagwu and Ezie (2013) submit that, despite the negativity associated with the operations of some multinational corporations in Nigeria, it has its positives as well. These positives come from the perceived contributions of multinational firms in the advancement of the country's technology, opening opportunities for sustained employment for the country's youthful population. In a similar line of argument, Kumar (2015) submits that "multinational companies (MNCs) play an important role in linking rich and poor economies and in transferring capital, knowledge, ideas and value systems across borders of different countries."

However, there have also been contestations as to the role of multinational corporations in the economic wellbeing of

"The Promises and Perils of Multinational Corporations: The Nigerian Experience," by Dan-Jumbo Comfort T. and Akpan Ekom Etim, International Journal of Management Science and Business Administration, March 2018. https://researchleap.com/promises-perils-multinational-corporations-nigerian-experience/. Licensed under CC BY 4.0 International.

countries. Odunlami and Awolusi (2015) noted that Multinational corporations are exploitative in nature, encourage capital flight and may pose threats to a country's laws and sovereignty. The controversies trailing the perceived benefits and/or damages of multinational enterprises in the world economy and in the Nigerian economy specifically, inform the need to explore the relationship between multinational corporations and economic development of the country. Therefore, this study is set to investigate the influence multinational corporations have on the economic development of Nigeria, based on extant literature.

Meaning and Evolution of Multinational Corporations

Multinational corporations comprise businesses operating or having business interests in more than one country, mostly headquartered in the parent country. There have been several definitions of multinational enterprise, which are also known as transnational corporations (Kumar, 2015). Lazarus (2001) defines a multinational corporation as a "business organization whose activities are located in more than two countries." Similarly, Dunning (1992) defined multinational enterprise as "an enterprise that engages in foreign direct investment and owns or controls value-adding activities in more than one country." In a more recent publication Kumar (2015) defines multinational corporations as "those large firms which are incorporated in one country but which own, control or manage production and distribution facilities in several countries." Therefore, multinational corporations are involved in the transactions of large volume of businesses. According to Udoka (2015) multinational corporations are organizations which operate strategically on an international scale. A multinational corporation is a company, firm or enterprise that operates worldwide with its headquarters in a metropolitan or developed country. Hill (2005) defines Multinational Enterprise as "any business that has productive activities in two or more countries."

All the definitions cited above suggest different distinct characteristics of multinational enterprise. Lazarus pointed out that, for a corporation to qualify to be called multinational, it must have functional offices in at least two countries. While, Dunning suggested that, the organization must be involved in foreign direct investment and should be operating not just in its parent country. Kumar supported this view. However, he noted that, they should have production facility or distribution channel in several countries. All the definitions seem to agree that, multinational corporations should be present in more than two countries.

The historical development of multinational companies in Nigeria can be traced as far back as the mid nineteenth century however they started to gain a lot of attention in the middle of the 20th century. According to Ajayi and Omolekan (2013), the genealogy of multinational corporations in Nigeria can be traced as far back as the colonial dispensation. United African Company, then known as Nigerian Motors Ltd, a subsidiary of the Royal Niger Company, was established by the British government and involved in the extraction of raw mineral resources (e.g. ore, coal), exporting the raw mineral and in the merchandising of general goods in the 1930s.

With the discovery of oil in the Niger Delta in the 1950s, there was influx of multinational corporations in the country. This was led by the Royal Deutch Company (Shell), the coming of these wealthy foreign companies into the country cannot be said to have not benefitted the country as the multinational corporations have provided jobs to thousands of youths in the country (Ajayi & Omolekan, 2013). As suggested by Abdul-Gafaru (2006), multinational corporations help in the development of local manpower through the transfer of knowledge, experience, technology which may not be available locally. However, contemporary social, political and economic discussions are awash with unsavoury tales about the activities of multinational corporations in the country. Some scholars, such as Onimode (1982) regard multinational corporations as "monsters that have consistently and systematically stultified economic development in various parts of the world." The deservingness vis-à-vis the demerits of multinational corporations in the economic development of the country is examined in this work.

Theories of Multinational Corporations

Several theories have been expounded to enunciate the activities and roles of multinational corporations. Such theories include but not limited to: "Eclectic Paradigm General Theory of Multinational Enterprises"—(Dunning, 1979; 1980; 1988); "Internalization (Transaction Cost) Theory of MNEs"—(Buckley & Casson, 1976); "Product Cycle Theory"—(Vernon, 1966; 1979); "Hymer-Kindleberger Theory"—(Hymer, 1960; Kindleberger, 1984, 1989); "The Aliber Theory"—(Aliber, 1970); "Location Theory of International Investment." However, in this work three theories that have been shown to have relevance to the relationship between multinational corporations and the economic development of Nigeria will be reviewed. These are: "New Trade Theory"— (Krugman, 1970); "Unequal Exchange Theory"—(Emmanuel, 1972); and "Dependency Theory"—(Prebisch, 1950).

The New Trade Theory
The New Trade Theory was developed in the 1970s by the notable scholar Paul Krugman. The basic assumption of the new trade theory is that every country has a comparative advantage over other countries if the country constantly produces a particular product or is known for rendering a specific service.

The New Trade Theory (NTT) was a notable departure from the more popular neoclassical economy theory. Its cardinal departure point was hinged on the fact that countries can achieve competitive advantage by producing what they know how to produce and continuously gaining experience by producing same product overtime (Sen, 2010). A related study by Eluka, Ndubuisi-Okolo and Anekwe (2016) pointed out that "a critical factor in determining international patterns of trade is the very substantial economies of scale and network effect that can occur in key industries. These economies of scale and network of effects can be so significant that they outweigh the more traditional theory of comparative advantage."

However, concerns have been raised by scholars pertaining the workability of the new trade theory (Sen, 2005), specifically, as it concerns the effect of firm size and market structure of the country. New trade theory is also said to encourage monopoly in a market and may discourage international corporations from doing business in a country adopting it. Nevertheless, new trade theory recognizes the importance of "scale economies, imperfect markets, and product differentiation" (Bhattacharjea, 2004; Sen, 2010).

Dependency Theory
The dependency theory was developed by Prebisch and his colleagues, at the United Nations Economic Commission for Latin America in the 1950s, who believed that economic advancement in the industrialized nations did not result in economic growth in the less industrialized business partners. In their research, they discovered that there was inverse relationship between the economic growth of the western countries and their less developed partner countries. As noted by Ferraro (1996), Prebisch's position negates the neoclassical theory, which theorized that the economic advancement of one country is advantageous to all countries (this is known as "pareto optimal"), though the reward may not be symmetrically distributed.

Prebisch's work compendiously captured the relationship between the developed countries and their poorer partners. This condition of relationship was aptly Ferraro (1996) as "poor countries exported primary commodities to the rich countries which then manufactured products out of those commodities and sold them back to the poorer countries. The value added by manufacturing a usable product always cost more than the primary products used to create those products. Therefore, poorer countries would never be earning enough from their export earnings to pay for their imports."

The dependency was defined by Sunkel (1969) as "as an explanation of the economic development of a state in terms of the external influences—political, economic, and cultural—on national development policies". Similarly, Dos Santos (1971) submitted that, dependency is a circumstance "which shapes a certain structure of the world economy such that it favours some countries to the detriment of others and limits the development possibilities of the subordinate economics," a condition which the economy of some countries is patterned by the advancement of a different country. That is, the development of one leads to the under-development of another.

The dependency theory sophists presuppose that there is no possibility of economic autonomy for a dependent state since they are continuously being underdeveloped by their more industrialized partners. The theorists are of the view that the less developed states should formulate and implement policies that will lead to less importation of goods, while still selling their products on the international market, this will help preserve their foreign exchange.

Unequal Exchange Theory
The continuously underdevelopment of third world countries by the Western countries motivated Arghiri Emmanuel to proposed the unequal exchange theory in 1972. According to Houston and Paus (1987) Emmanuel's unequal theory precisely describe "the proportion between equilibrium prices that is established through the equalization of profits between regions in which the rate of surplus value is institutionally different. Since the differences in rates of surplus value are the direct result of wage differentials, inequality of wages as such, all other things being equal, is alone the cause of the inequality of exchange."

Though there have much criticism of the Emmanuel's hypothesis that "unequal exchange" is accountable for the underdevelopment of the third world countries (e.g. Gibson, 1980; Foot & Webber, 1983; Houston & Paus, 1987). Houston and Paus (1987) recommended a total abandonment of this theory, since they proposed that the idea of equal exchange is not achievable and that unequal exchange cannot be used to explain disproportionate development among partner nations. However in recent studies (e.g. Eluka, et al., 2016), this theory has been used to explain the underdevelopment of dependent countries. As in the case of Nigeria where the county exports it crude oil and other natural resources at a very cheap rate to the multinational companies who took it out to refine and sell the refined products back to the country at exorbitant prices.

All the theories discussed shared common fundamental characteristics that the development of one country is at the expense of another. Therefore, all countries especially the less development states should strive to be self-sufficient for its basic and endeavor to export more goods than they import. The applicability and relevance of these theories to the Nigerian situation is discussed in the following paragraphs.

Multinational Corporations and Economic Development in Nigeria

Since the independence of Nigeria in 1960 from it colonial masters (England) the country has witnessed a 'zig-zag' like kind of development. The country is still ranked as a developing country despite its enormous natural endowments; and her contemporaries (e.g. India, Singapore) having advanced their economies to enviable levels. The underdevelopment of the country, it is largely claimed, is partly caused by the exploitative nature of multinational firms operating in the country (e.g. Irogbe, 2013; Eluka, et al., 2016). Irogbe (2013) authoritatively puts it that "MNCs, whose goal is the maximization of profits, are not philanthropic institutions and they serve the interests of no one but themselves." This opinion capture the whole essence of the negativity associated with multinational corporations in Nigeria. Likewise, Eluka, et al (2016) state that multinational corporations are "in the habit of employing expatriates to fill in the key positions. That is why they adopt the ethnocentric model of staff selection where expatriates are given preference in terms of recruitment and selection. This is inimical to the economic growth and development."

However, some authors have differing opinions. They maintained that multinational corporations help in the creation of working opportunities for the host country citizens (Tirimba & Macharia, 2014). They also proposed that multinationals alleviate the technological know-how of the host country through the transfer of knowledge from the expatriate workers to the local employees. Similarly, defenders of multinationals opined that multinational corporations act as engines of development to their host communities (Roach, 2007). Multinational firms are believed to enhance growth and development of their host countries and reduce the reliance on export goods which leads to higher level of competitiveness of the host countries' economies, resulting in efficiency and self-sufficiency in the long-run (Bakare, 2010; Odunlami & Awolusi, 2015).

Conclusion and Policy Recommendations

There have been several arguments that multinational corporations contribute enormously to the underdevelopment of developing such as Nigeria. However, the review above shows that most developing countries also derive some gains from the presence of multinational companies in their domain. Drawing strength from the dependency theory, Nigeria been a dependent state, stands no chance of development unless conscious steps are taken to move the country from being a dependent state to a producing state.

Therefore, it is recommended that:

- Steps should be taken to encourage local manufacturers through the provision of conducive operating environment for them to operate and compete favourably with foreign counterparts.

- Basic amenities/social infrastructure such as roads, electricity, pipe-borne water should be put in place in order to reduce the cost of doing business in Nigeria.
- There should be tax waivers for young local producers.
- Government should also help in the provision of start-up capital for fresh graduates who are willing to venture into manufacturing.

The Human and Environmental Costs of Multinational Corporations

Jade Vasquez

Jade Vasquez served as a research associate for the Council on Hemispheric Affairs (COHA).

A t an October 5 conference hosted by the nonprofit, Resources for the Future, economist Joseph E. Stiglitz stated, "We now know why the invisible hand is invisible: because it is often not there." The Columbia University professor supported this claim by noting that the people with the fewest means pay the highest price in this increasingly unbalanced globalized world. Some prominent examples of groups who have suffered enormously from corporate exploitation are the indigenous tribes of the Ecuadorian Amazon. Rich in wildlife and natural resources, the tropical rainforest, known to natives as the *Oriente,* has provided its inhabitants with a vital foundation of food and water for millennia, while fostering a cultural heritage unlike any other in the world. Indigenous tribes, including the Cofán, Secoya, Kicha and Huarani peoples, lived traditional lifestyles completely untouched by modern civilization, until 1964, when US oil firm Texaco discovered oil in the northern region of the Ecuadorian jungle.[1]

For 28 years, Texaco, bought out by Chevron in 2001, made cost-cutting operational decisions that contaminated the Amazon's rivers and polluted among the world's most treasured ecosystem.[2] The oil giant's negligent drilling practices have left natives to suffer from an array of deplorable health complications, an erosion of their culture, and quite possibly, the planet's worst ongoing environmental disaster. The 1990s was a historical period for Ecuadorian indigenous groups, as they finally joined forces to

"An End to Corporate Impunity: Making Chevron Accountable for Environmental Disaster," by Jade Vasquez, Council on Hemispheric Affairs (COHA), November 6, 2012. http://www.coha.org/an-end-to-corporate-impunity-making-chevron-accountable-for-environmental-disaster/. Licensed under CC BY-ND 4.0 International.

combat corporate exploitation, building a lawsuit against present-day Chevron that exposed the company for its detrimental impact on Amazonian communities. After decades of court cases and appeals, the legal battle is finally coming to a close, with a defeated Chevron required to pay an unprecedented $19 billion USD to Ecuador's most affected victims.[3] Struggling to discover new loopholes in the case, Chevron may finally be forced to suffer the consequences of its own actions, respecting a ruling that in the future could make multinational corporations accountable for their environmental and human rights abuses around the globe.

Oil Giant Stomps Through Vulnerable Territory

Amazonian natives had no idea what to expect when oil workers entered their land and founded Lago Agrio, a town named after Texaco's birthplace in Sour Lake, Texas, nearly fifty years ago.[4] Similarly, the Ecuadorian government was unaware of the forthcoming catastrophic damages Texaco would impose on their prized rainforest, as the oil giant was the first US company to drill for oil in the Amazon. Trusting the corporation's modern oil practices and technological initiatives, Ecuador's national oil company, Petroecuador, united with Texaco to form *Texpet*, creating a toxic relationship between corrupt government officials and corporate representatives. This relationship was especially lethal during the remediation period, in which Chevron claims to have spent $40 million USD in what plaintiffs call a "sham" clean up.[5] Nevertheless, before the oil company left Ecuador in 1992 and began fulfilling the 1995 Remediation Action agreement, much of the damage had already been done. Unlike other oil spills, where billions of gallons of crude were spilled during one event, Texaco's cheaply designed extraction complex of 350 wells led to "extreme systematic pollution and exposure to toxins from multiple sources on a daily basis for nearly three decades," according to ChevronToxico, an organization campaigning for Ecuadorian justice.[6]

In a recent statement, Chevron representatives declared that the company "is defending itself against the false allegation that it is responsible for alleged environmental and social harms in the Amazon region of Ecuador," claiming that its subsidiary, Texaco, fully remediated its share of environmental impacts arising from oil production prior to its departure.[7] Despite receiving a release of liability from negligent government officials, Texaco left behind over 900 open toxic waste pits; a number of which the company claims is the responsibility of Petroecuador.[8] However, Chevron cannot place all of the blame on Petroecuador, as the oil giant itself admitted to dumping over 16 billion gallons of cancer-causing production waters, a byproduct of the drilling process, into the streams of the *Oriente*. Thus, in order to save funds, Texaco chose to use illegal environmental practices that contaminated the Amazon waterways and harmed many of the 30,000 people who depend on the tainted waters for drinking, cooking, bathing, cleaning, and fishing.[9]

The rivers' black blankets, as the locals like to call them, are only one of the many notorious legacies Texaco left behind in Ecuador's jungle. Along with the dumping of production waters and the abandonment of unlined waste pits, Chevron never even developed a plan to contain and clean up its frequent oil spills and in the process destroyed numerous documents that mentioned any of the hazardous ruptures. Additionally, according to the Amazon Defense Coalition's "Summary of Overwhelming Evidence Against Chevron in Ecuador Trial," "…Chevron exclusively used poorly maintained flares to burn natural gas that caused extensive air pollution… Texaco routinely burned off oil from pits and spills, contaminating the air with huge plumes of black smoke."[10] For nearly thirty years, the crude operator violated countless laws designed to protect the Amazon's ecosystem and the health of its inhabitants, perpetuating the contamination and depriving natives of the resources they depend on daily for survival.

Contaminated Water Causes Cancer and Other Diseases Among Indigenous

Beyond contaminating the environment, oil extraction in the Amazon has also had a detrimental impact on the health of the rainforest's residents, polluting the soil and waterways with toxins and carcinogens. According to Richard Cabrera, a geological engineer appointed by the Ecuadorian court, of the $18 billion USD that Amazonian communities originally demanded, $9 billion should go to conducting an extensive clean-up, along with the development of new health and water systems. The other half should go to compensate cancer deaths.[11] Although this number may seem overwhelming, plaintiffs have argued it is still pennies on the dollar, considering that Chevron earned billions from the project, while its substandard operational practices decimated the local population.

According to Ecuador's National Cancer Registry, from 1985 to 2000, over 1200 cases of cancer were reported from provinces in oil-producing regions, including Sucumbios, Orellana, Napo, and Pastaza.[12] Because the Amazon does not have its own cancer registry, this number only reflects the cases that were referred to Quito, excluding the affected victims that do not have the means to travel to a healthcare facility. Based on a 2004 study by Miguel San Sebastian and Ana-Karin Hurtig, cancer incidents were significantly higher among men and women living in oil-exploited provinces than in any other Ecuadorian region, with men suffering from cancers of the stomach, rectum, skin melanoma, soft tissue, and kidneys and women suffering from cancer of the cervix and lymph nodes.[13] With billions of gallons of untreated toxic waste, gas, and oil released into the environment, it is difficult to label the increasing rate of disease in the Amazon as a coincidence.

Many indigenous parents have had to perform the devastating task of burying their children at a very young age. Pregnant women exposed to the Amazon's toxins frequently suffer from miscarriages, and many of the children who live through the tumultuous pregnancies are born with a range of birth defects, reducing their chances of survival in this highly polluted jungle. Childhood leukemia is especially prevalent in the dreary rainforest. According to San Sebastian and Hurtig's report "Incidence of Childhood Leukemia and Oil Exploitation in the Amazon Basin of

Ecuador," studies found elevated rates of leukemia among children between the ages of zero and 14 in oil contaminated areas.[14] Making matters worse for the victims, Ecuador's oil-producing regions contain few healthcare facilities, providing minimal services that lack chemotherapy treatment for cancer patients.[15] Due to geographic isolation, poor infrastructure, and socioeconomic status, Amazonians are severely limited in their access to adequate healthcare, leaving a sense of hopelessness for parents and their children in this disease-prone society.

Indigenous Solidarity Brings Chevron to Trial

Enraged from having to prematurely bury their own people beneath the dark jungle, indigenous groups, along with environmental human rights organizations, decided to seek justice. In 1993, 30,000 Ecuadorians filed a class action lawsuit against Texaco, which Chevron inherited when the two companies merged in 2001.[16] Organizations such as Amazon Watch, Amazon Defense Coalition, and the Confederation of Indigenous Nationalities of Ecuador (CONAIE), Ecuador's strongest indigenous union, supported the Amazonian settlers in their quest for justice. For the next twenty years, these organizations would use activism and media pressure to ensure that the corporate criminal fulfills its moral obligation to the devastated land and people it left behind.

Texaco stalled the trial for ten years after a US judge granted the company's request to move the case from New York to Lago Agrio. The manipulative change of the trial's location was the company's first of many delaying tactics that prevented a resolution for the rainforest's indigenous communities. As the years passed, and Texaco continued to use its influence to obstruct justice, more and more Ecuadorians died of pollution-related diseases. When the case reopened in 2003, present-day Chevron did not have the good fortune of being granted a jury, as they would have in New York, but were instead at the mercy of one Ecuadorian judge, Juan Nuñez. The judge's nationality led to a series of controversies, with Silvia Garrigo, manager of Chevron Global Issues and Policy, stating that the court's experts and judge were biased and prone to fraud due to the country's corrupt politicized judicial system.[17]

Chevron's attack on Ecuador's court system became a common theme throughout the trial, with Chevron lawyer Adolfo Callejas arguing in his opening statement that the Ecuadorian court had no jurisdiction to try the case. It was believed that Chevron could not be sued because of the 1995 Ecuadorian agreement that released Texaco of liability. However, according to the plaintiffs' lead American lawyer, Steven Donzinger, "Our clients never released Texaco. That is the critical distinction. That was an agreement between the government and Texaco. We are not part of that agreement and we are not bound by that agreement."[18] Chevron's righteous corporate attitude is the reason why indigenous groups never believed they had the right to sue an American company on Ecuadorian soil. In March 2011, however, indigenous doubts were reversed, after the Ecuadorian judgment ordered Chevron to pay the victorious Amazonians a historic $19 billion USD.[19] After a year and several attempts to block the global judgment and with the US Supreme court denying their bid, Chevron is finally being forced to surrender their assets to their most affected victims.

The Chevron Ecuador case is a landmark victory for indigenous groups everywhere. The verdict against Chevron has produced a number of positive implications for other poor indigenous citizens of the developing world. The devastation of the Amazon is a testament to Stiglitz's remark that an unregulated market mainly hurts society's most vulnerable people. However, the Amazonians' success throughout the legal process exposes the invisible hand for all its ethical violations and brings exploitative corporations, like Chevron, to justice. Nevertheless, this unprecedented victory does not ease the pain the indigenous have suffered and will continue to endure in the next several years. Families continue to bury their loved ones, as severe health complications persist from the pollution, and despite the seizure of Chevron's assets, Ecuador continues to propose new extractive projects that harm the environment and the people in it.

The Ecuadorian government, who relies heavily on oil for economic development, must make responsible decisions in regards to future extractive projects. Examples of this kind of prudent governance include the Palacio Administration's 2006 efforts with indigenous and conservation groups to prevent the Brazilian national oil company, Petrobras, from building a road through the Amazon.[20] Furthermore, the government must make healthcare more accessible to everyone while taking greater precautionary measures for environmental disasters. Although globalization has led to the environmental degradation of the Amazon and severe health complications of its inhabitants, Ecuador remains a viable economic player in the region. However, government officials must focus its attention on environmental sustainability and social justice if it wants to maintain an economic security that benefits all of its citizens.

Sources

[1] Chevron Toxico. "A Rainforest Chernobyl." Accessed October 15, 2012. http://chevrontoxico.com/about/rainforest-chernobyl/.

[2] IBID.

[3] "Supreme Court Denies Chevron $19bn Ecuador Appeal." *BBC News*. October 9, 2012. http://www.bbc.co.uk/news/world-us-canada-19892561.

[4] Chevron Toxico. "A Rainforest Chernobyl." Accessed October 15, 2012. http://chevrontoxico.com/about/rainforest-chernobyl/.

[5] Chevron Public Affairs. "Texpet's Remediation and Revegetation of Oilfield Pits in the Ecuadorian Amazon." Accessed October 14, 2012. http://www.texaco.com/sitelets/ecuador/docs/texaco_ecuador_remediation_en.pdf

[6] Chevron Toxico. "A Rainforest Chernobyl." Accessed October 15, 2012. http://chevrontoxico.com/about/rainforest-chernobyl/.

[7] Chevron. "The Facts About Chevron in Ecuador and the Plaintiffs' Strategy of Fraud." January 2012. http://www.chevron.com/documents/pdf/ecuador/ecuador-lawsuit-fact-sheet.pdf.

[8] Amazon Defense Coalition. "Understanding Chevron's 'Amazon Chernobyl.'" Feburary 1, 2009. http://www.texacotoxico.org/eng/node/143.

[9] *Amazon Crude*. 60 Minutes. Performed by Scott Pelley. 2009. New York: CBS News, Medium. See also "Summary of Overwhelming Evidence Against Chevron in Ecuador Trial." Amazon Defense Coalition. January 2012. http://chevrontoxico.com/assets/docs/2012-01-evidence-summary.pdf.

[10] "Summary of Overwhelming Evidence Against Chevron in Ecuador Trial." Amazon Defense Coalition. January 2012. http://chevrontoxico.com/assets/docs/2012-01-evidence-summary.pdf.

[11] *Amazon Crude.* 60 Minutes. Performed by Scott Pelley. 2009. New York: CBS News, Medium.

[12] Sociedad de Lucha contra el Cáncer. Cáncer en regiones del Ecuador. Quito, Ecuador: SOLCA, 2001.

[13] San Sebastián, Miguel and Anna-Karin Hurtig. "Oil Exploitation in the Amazon Basin of Ecuador: A Public Health Emergency." *Rev Panam Salud Publica/ Pan Am Public Health.* 15.3 (2004): 205-211. http://www.texacotoxico.org/eng/sites/default/files/Public_Health_Emergency_RPSP%20%28ENG%29.pdf.

[14] San Sebastián, Miguel and Anna-Karin Hurtig. "Incidence if Childhood Leukemia and Oil Exploitation in the Amazon Basin of Ecuador." *International Journal of Occupational and Environmental Health.* 10.3 (2004): 245-250. http://www.texacotoxico.org/eng/sites/default/files/ChildhoodLeukemia.pdf.

[15] San Sebastián, Miguel and Anna-Karin Hurtig. "Oil Exploitation in the Amazon Basin of Ecuador: A Public Health Emergency." *Rev Panam Salud Publica/ Pan Am Public Health.* 15.3 (2004): 205-211. http://www.texacotoxico.org/eng/sites/default/files/Public_Health_Emergency_RPSP%20%28ENG%29.pdf.

[16] *Crude: The Real Price of Oil.* Directed by Joe Berlinger. 2009. New York, NY: First Run Features, 2010. DVD.

[17] *Amazon Crude.* 60 Minutes. Performed by Scott Pelley. 2009. New York: CBS News, Medium.

[18] IBID.

[19] "U.S. Supreme Court Squelches Chevron Appeal on Ecuador Case." *The Chevron Pit.* October 9, 2012. http://thechevronpit.blogspot.mx/2012/10/us-supreme-court-squelches-chevron.html.

[20] "Petrobras Abandons Plans for Oil Road in Ecuadorian Amazon Park." *Environment News Service.* April 24, 2006. http://www.ens-newswire.com/ens/sep2005/2005-09-08-01.asp.

Multinational Corporations Standards of Living in Developing Countries

James C. W. Ahiakpor

James Ahiakpor is professor of economics at California State University and author of multiple books, articles, and reviews. He received his PhD in economics from the University of Toronto.

Multinational corporations (MNCs) engage in very useful and morally defensible activities in Third World countries for which they frequently have received little credit. Significant among these activities are their extension of opportunities for earning higher incomes as well as the consumption of improved quality goods and services to people in poorer regions of the world. Instead, these firms have been misrepresented by ugly or fearful images by Marxists and "dependency theory" advocates. Because many of these firms originate in the industrialized countries, including the US, the UK, Canada, Germany, France, and Italy, they have been viewed as instruments for the imposition of Western cultural values on Third World countries, rather than allies in their economic development. Thus, some proponents of these views urge the expulsion of these firms, while others less hostile have argued for their close supervision or regulation by Third World governments.

Incidents such as the improper use in the Third World of baby milk formula manufactured by Nestle, the gas leak from a Union Carbide plant in Bhopal, India, and the alleged involvement of foreign firms in the overthrow of President Allende of Chile have been used to perpetuate the ugly image of MNCs. The fact that some MNCs command assets worth more than the national income of their host countries also reinforces their fearful image.

"Multinational Corporations in the Third World: Predators or Allies in Economic Development?" by James C. W. Ahiakpor, Acton Institute, July 20, 2010. Reprinted by permission.

And indeed, there is evidence that some MNCs have paid bribes to government officials in order to get around obstacles erected against profitable operations of their enterprises.

Several governments, especially in Latin America and Africa, have been receptive to the negative images and have adopted hostile policies towards MNCs. However, a careful examination of the nature of MNCs and their operations in the Third World reveals a positive image of them, especially as the allies in the development process of these countries. For the greater well-being of the majority of the world's poor who live in the Third World, it is important that the positive contributions of these firms to their economies become more widely known. Even as MNCs may be motivated primarily by profits to invest in the Third World, the morality of their activities in improving the material lives of many in these countries should not be obscured through misperceptions.

The first point to recognize about MNCs is that, besides operating under more than one sovereign jurisdiction, they are in nature very similar to local or non-multinational firms producing in more than one state or plant. We may call such multi-plant firms uninational corporations (UNCs). Thus, a UNC with branch plants in Alaska as well as some other parts of the US would have been known as an MNC had Alaska continued to be a non-US territory. Indeed, the experience of European countries soon to become more unified economically or the former Soviet Union now breaking up into several sovereign or quasi-sovereign states should impress us of the fact that the United States or Canada easily could have been several independent countries, and some present UNCs would have been MNCs.

Like UNCs, MNCs are owned by shareholders who expect annual returns or dividends in compensation for funds they make available for the firm's production and sales activities. It is to enable MNCs to pay such dividends that their managers seek out the most efficient workers for the wages they pay, buy materials at the cheapest costs possible, seek to produce in countries levying the lowest profit taxes, and sell in markets where they can earn the highest revenues after costs. (This is no different from anyone seeking employment at the highest wage for the least amount of tedium, the most congenial work environment and location, and the highest employment benefits.) Perhaps the main difference between uninational and multinational corporations is that the latter have been more successful than the former, and as a result have expanded their activities to many more regions and sovereign states.

Many do recognize UNCs or local firms as helpful agents in the development of the communities in which they operate. Primary in this recognition is the employment they create and the (higher) incomes earned because of their having established in the region. These firms also rent buildings and land, or sometimes buy them, thus generating higher incomes for their owners. For example, in the absence of the present Japanese owners having bid for the Rockefeller Center in New York, the price its American owners would have gotten for it would have been lower. The same applies to the income prospects of owners of the Seattle Mariners should the sale of this club to the Japanese buyers go through. It is precisely in similar ways that MNCs enrich labor and other resource owners in the Third World. In their absence, the people would have had fewer or much lower paying jobs, and the demand for land and other local resources would have been lower. Without the operators of such hotels as the Holiday Inn, the Sheraton, the Hyatt, Four Seasons, and the Hilton having leased or bought beach-front properties in several of the popular tourist resorts in the Third World, their owners (individuals or government) might have received much less for their sale. Such purchases also release the capital of resource owners for investment in other enterprises.

Some of those who recognize little positive contributions from MNCs to the economics development of the Third World countries might, however, acknowledge that these firms pay higher wages to local employees than they typically would receive elsewhere, and higher rents for land and buildings. But they often argue that the wages in Third World countries are lower than those paid by MNCs in the more developed countries, and the working conditions are not of the same standard. However, the comparison misses several key points. For example, the skill or educational levels of workers in the Third World and those of the more developed countries are not the same. The amount of machinery and equipment handled by workers in the two locations are also different. In short, the amount of output generated by a worker in the Third World is typically smaller than that produced in the more developed world. Indeed, if MNCs could hire enough of higher skilled workers in the more developed countries at the wages workers are paid in the Third World, they would gladly do so. They would thus earn higher profits while selling their goods and services at lower prices. But the fact is that the voluntary exchange system in which MNCs operate would not permit them. Besides those working for charity, few others would for long accept wages they consider to be less than their contribution to an enterprise.

The same explanation applies to wages paid by MNCs in the Third World. Unless workers find it most profitable to work for MNCs at the wages they offer, they would choose employment elsewhere. Similarly, unless MNCs can make as much profit as they can at home, as well as compensation for the additional risks taken to invest in the Third World, including the risk of asset confiscation by a hostile future government, they would not venture into those parts of the world. Thus, there have to be net benefits for both parties in a transaction (here workers and multinational corporations) for the transaction to take place, and on a continuous basis.

It may also be worthwhile to point out that research has not confirmed the frequent assertion that foreign firms, including MNCs, make excessive or higher profits per dollar invested than their local counterparts. On the contrary, private local firms on average earn higher rates of profits before taxes than foreign firms (as revealed by research in India, Brazil, Columbia, Guatemala, Ghana, and Kenya). And the simple explanation is that many Third World governments tax the profits of their local firms than they do those of foreign firms. Thus, the after-tax rates of profit are similar for foreign and private local firms in the Third World. Furthermore, new wealth created by any firm has to cover the wages, interest, equipment, and the rental costs of land and buildings incurred in production before profits are paid. And much of such payments stay within the host Third World economy.

If we withhold our paternalistic instincts towards poorer people in the Third World, we would also respect their judgement to purchase products manufactured there by MNCs rather than accuse the firms of selling inappropriate products to them. Being poor does not make one's choice of products less defensible or moral than the choices of the rich. And without sufficient demand for the products, MNCs would not make profits from selling them in the Third World. In a free trading regime, the same products might have been imported had they not been produced by MNCs. There is thus no valid reason why Third World governments should require that MNCs manufacture and sell only second- or third-rate quality products in those countries, as some analysts from the more developed countries have suggested. Is there anything legitimate that Third World governments can do about the activities of multinational corporations in their countries? Yes; but nothing more than they legitimately and reasonably would do about local firms, bearing in mind that excessive taxation of profits or environmental regulations reduce total investments by both types of firms. Perhaps, MNCs may be able to offer bigger bribes than local firms to escape restrictions imposed on them by Third World governments. If so, such restrictions mainly work against the development of local firms. The solution ought to be a loosening of restrictions on businesses so they may create more wealth and in the process facilitate the development of local enterprise and lessen the incidence of corruption in government.

Adam Smith, who was also a moral philosopher, long observed that an individual "by directing . . . industry in such a manner as its produce may be of the greatest value, . . . intends only his own gain, and he is in this, as in many other cases, led by an invisible hand to promote an end which was no part of it. By pursuing his own interest he frequently promotes that of the society more effectually than when he really intends to promote it." These observations apply with equal force to the investment activities of multinational corporations in Third World countries. And it is no accident that people in those Third World countries whose governments have been more open to the presence of multinational corporations have experienced significant improvements in their standard of living (e.g., Bermuda, the Bahamas, Hong Kong, South Korea, Singapore, and Taiwan) while many in countries hostile to these firms continue to be mired in poverty. It may not be the intent of Third World governments, but perpetuating poverty in the name of protecting their people from alleged exploitation by MNCs has little moral justification.

Low Wages in Developing Countries Are Due to Low Productivity, Not Exploitation

Art Carden

Art Carden is associate professor of economics at Samford University and a senior research fellow with the Institute for Faith, Work, and Economics, a senior fellow with the Beacon Center of Tennessee, and a research fellow with the Independent Institute.

L ow wages in developing countries are among the many sins allegedly committed by global capitalism, but few of those making the charge really stop to think about why wages are so low in some developing countries.

In his 2007 book *The Myth of the Rational Voter*, economist Bryan Caplan proposes an interesting thought experiment which suggests that people implicitly accept the results of competitive markets. Caplan asks if those who criticize companies that pay low wages overseas feel that they could get rich quick by investing all of their resources in overseas enterprises—specifically, enterprises in poor countries. After all, it stands to reason that if workers in developing countries are underpaid and exploited, a profit-seeking businessperson would be able to reap immediate profits by hiring the workers away from their current occupations and re-employing them elsewhere.

If people pass on the opportunity, Caplan argues, then they implicitly accept the tragic-but-nonetheless-real fact that workers in very poor countries simply are not very productive. Low wages, then, are not the product of exploitative multinational corporations but of extremely low productivity. The relevant question for those concerned about the very poor is not "how do we convince (or force) multinational corporations to pay more" but "how can we improve the productivity of the world's poorest workers?"

This is where there is room for improvement, and this improvement should come by improving contracting institutions in poor countries. I don't have the specific local or cultural knowledge to know exactly how these institutions will evolve, but socially conscious investors or activists should try to encourage the development of institutions that constrain coercion and limit fraud.

Suffice it to say that the strategy of blocking overseas investment is ineffective at its best and positively harmful at its worst. I'm willing to grant the possibility that global labor markets are monopsonistic rather than competitive, but international capital flows suggest that this is not the case.

In a study of wages and working conditions in developing countries, economists Benjamin Powell and David Skarbek found that the textile sweatshops derided by rich westerners offer higher wages and better working conditions than the alternatives in very poor countries. People in developing countries need more sweatshops rather than fewer.

On the domestic front, people have argued that they are for "free trade" but that environmental standards should be improved so as to ensure that workers in poor countries are not exploited and their environments pillaged. But this eliminates poor workers' competitive advantage, reduces the possible gains from trade, and relegates them to an underground labor market of prostitution or picking through garbage dumps.

Regulation also will not change the productivity of very poor workers. It will only change the incentives, and this will likely produce unwanted consequences. Environmental regulation and onerous labor laws will alter the incentives in such a way as to increase the relative profitability of evading the law, tilting the competitive balance in favor of the relatively unscrupulous.

"That might be true," people might respond, "but can't multibillion-dollar multinational corporations afford to pay more? Isn't it unconscionable that CEOs are able to take home millions while workers in underdeveloped countries earn mere cents per hour?"

Is it sad? Yes. Is it unconscionable? No. Can companies "afford to pay more?" Again, the answer is no. Firms might be able to pay above-market wages in the short run, but in addition to operating in internationally competitive labor markets they also operate in internationally competitive capital markets and internationally competitive goods markets. Firms that sacrifice profits in order to pay higher wages will reduce their ability to earn profits, attract capital, and expand in the future. In the short run, we can improve standards of living for some people. In the long run, this illusory prosperity comes at the cost of increasing future poverty.

The current crisis faced by American automakers provides a useful and tragic case in point. For years, they were able to pay some workers at union pay scales with union benefits. Over time, however, they were undercut by competitors who were unhampered by these costly restrictions and they were themselves sharply restricted in their ability to expand. Now, apparently, there isn't anything left to loot.

"People in developing countries need more sweatshops rather than fewer."

Finally, when it comes to a firm's production decisions, wages are not all that matters. Firms will invest in inputs—say "unskilled labor" and "skilled labor"—until the ratio of the marginal products of the factors to the prices of the factors are equal for all inputs. If an American worker earns $30 per hour while a Chinese worker earns $1 per hour, this is not by itself sufficient to show that investing in China is in a firm's best interests. If the American worker can produce 120 units of output in an hour while the Chinese worker can only produce two, then producing the good in the United States is actually cheaper. Each unit produced in the United States costs twenty-five cents, while each unit produced in China costs fifty cents.

The idea that expanding and integrating the global marketplace exploits the poor is a myth that causes avoidable misery. Protesting and trying to slow the advance of international capitalism is not the solution. Encouraging the development of institutions in which the world's poor can increase their productivity is.

Sweatshops Provide Essential Economic Opportunities for Developing Countries

Annabelle Wong

Annabelle Wong is a graduate of the National University of Singapore with a master's degree in political science and government.

M any aspects of the average American's material lifestyle can be attributed to trade relations between the United States and Asia. A significant proportion of the clothes they wear, the toys they grew up with, and even the technology they use, was produced somewhere in Asia. Commerce with major developing nations like China and Indonesia is reportedly crucial for America's own continued economic prosperity, since its overall manufacturing investments in developing nations are in tens of billions of dollars and huge numbers of plants there operate on a contract basis with American companies. However, many Americans are unaware that their appetite for consumerism fuels a deeply controversial industry, and just as foreign-manufactured goods are often more than meets the eye, the sweatshop debate is highly intricate.

The definition of a sweatshop remains broad, describing any factory which may have unreasonably authoritative overseers, dangerous and unhealthy (both physically and psychologically) working conditions, and enforces long hours with low pay. The term also frequently describes a factory employing child labor. Many developed nations, including the United States, have at some point engaged sweatshop production facilities on a large scale, and a major segment of the world's remaining sweatshops are located in Asia. As the West continues its long-standing tradition of fostering what many would liken to slave labor, an ethical examination of these business practices becomes increasingly important.

"Two Faces of Economic Development: The Ethical Controversy Surrounding U.S.-Related Sweatshops in Developing Asian Countries," by Annabelle Wong, Carnegie Council's Global Ethics Network, May 1, 2013. Reprinted by permission.

From a business perspective, sweatshops are overwhelmingly lucrative since they capitalize on low-wage labor in developing countries and significantly reduce production costs. Many major clothing and footwear companies, for example, have been linked to sweatshops. Brands such as Nike, GAP, Converse and Levi's, have all been guilty of numerous violations of requirements for reasonable working conditions in their production facilities. All of their headquarters and customer bases are located in the United States, while the manufacturing component of the production process is carried out in Asia. Such companies have been criticized as being complicit in the exploitation of workers because they fail to correct the manufacturers' malpractices, of which they are aware but often claim are hard to correct. An internal report carried out by Nike, for instance, found that nearly two-thirds of the 168 factories making Converse (one of the company's brands) products failed to meet Nike's own standards for manufacturing.

Sweatshops: The Ugly Face of Industrialization

One of the biggest hallmarks of sweatshop labor is that the workers are simply underpaid, especially considering the kinds of working conditions they endure. Minimum wage levels in countries such as Thailand, the Philippines, and China, are significantly lower than that of the United States. The federal minimum wage per hour in the United States is currently at 7.25 dollars, while it is 1.48 dollars in Thailand, 69 cents in the Philippines, and 67 cents in China. However, workers are frequently paid less than these estimates suggest—amounts barely enough to survive on even considering the lower cost of living in these regions. Many developing Asian countries have official minimum wage levels, but the lack of uniform and comprehensive regulations with nationwide coverage across all labor groups and industries remains a huge problem. For instance, minimum wage regulations are applicable in Cambodia only to the garment and shoe-sewing sector, and in Sri Lanka only to over 35 industrial trades. Furthermore, the lack of institutional regulatory effectiveness in enforcing compliance is an even greater problem.

Since turnover is extremely rapid, sweatshop workers are not guaranteed these meager salaries over the long term. For example, the International Textile, Garment and Leather Workers' Federation (ITGLWF) investigated a factory in Indonesia and found that over 80% of their workers were on short term contracts. Such factories hire and fire workers as volatile production needs change, with little regard for their employees' job security or welfare. These workers have no financial security to speak of, and also reported they did not get any sort of severance pay. In addition, these laborers are also subjected to violence, another common aspect of sweatshop operations in the developing world. Workers at a Converse plant in Sukabumi, Indonesia, reported that their supervisors threw shoes at them, slapped, kicked, and called them dogs and pigs. It is hard to measure the frequency and severity of physical and verbal abuse in these settings, as fear deters workers from reporting such cases and there is a characteristic lack of supervision. Furthermore, many sweatshop workers are children; roughly one in eight children in the Asia-Pacific is between the ages of 4 and 15 and works in a sweatshop. India has the highest rates of child labor of any country in the world, employing over 55 million children, many of whom were sold into labor by their families.

A Case for Sweatshops?

Despite the projected expansion of sweatshop operations, the harsh working conditions associated with it are frowned upon by the average person in the developed world. About a decade ago, a movement to boycott sweatshops became prominent in mainstream culture, with protests demanding that large US corporations stop buying and selling goods that came from extraneous, dangerous, underage and under-paid labor. Kathie Lee Gifford's clothing line for Wal-Mart is a prominent example; when it was discovered to be produced by sweatshops, activists in the United States expressed their disgust and Wal-Mart cut all ties with the manufacturers, essentially closing down the factories supplying that line. It appeared to be a victory for human rights, yet the Chinese immigrant workers who had been paid little or no wages for their 60-80 hours of toil each week, were outraged. Workers have consistently expressed concerns at the closing of even the most dismal sweatshops, and the constant and ready supply of sweatshop labor can be attributed to the fact that developing Asian countries and their peoples are in dire *need* of these economic opportunities, which outweighs their aversion to exploitative working conditions. Is the negative reaction in the developed world to sweatshops and their ethical violations essentially misinformed?

Some of the world's leading economists have cited sweatshops as a necessary step in modernization and development. Jeffrey D. Sachs of Harvard and Paul Krugman of the Massachusetts Institute of Technology have asserted that sweatshop manufacturing— especially in the production of goods like clothing and shoes— for foreign markets are an essential preliminary move toward economic prosperity in developing countries. Many credit these labor-intensive industries for propelling the Asian Tigers (Hong Kong, South Korea, Singapore and Taiwan) into the economically developed world. A study on poverty relief and development by the University of Santiago de Compostela also suggests that such sustainable international investment in low income countries is important to economic progress. America's sizeable investments in developing Asian countries represent not only investments in production facilities, but also add to the latter's investible resources and capital formation, transfer production technology, skills, innovative capacity, organizational and managerial practices, as well as provide access to international marketing networks, all of which are exceedingly helpful to these developing economies.

Are sweatshops a necessary evil, and what should the governments of the United States and developing Asian countries do?

A Conflict of Interests

Having personally witnessed the conditions in sweatshops and despite opposing the exploitation of workers, Harvard economist Jeffrey Sachs still claims that many nations have no better hope for economic progress than such manufacturing facilities which pay mere subsistence wages. He asserts that these jobs were the stepping stone for Singapore and Hong Kong, and are necessary to alleviate rural poverty in places like Africa. Does this mean that the moral outrage at sweatshop labor is unfounded? More importantly: what are the morally acceptable limits to the various types of costs incurred by the pursuit of economic progress and material well-being? There are no easy answers, but the first step to addressing these concerns involves identifying the relevant moral agents and their respective goals. Three key groups include:

1. *The governments of the United States and developing Asian countries:* They are responsible for protecting the interests of their peoples, including but not limited to their fundamental human rights and material well-being.

2. *US corporate businesses which employ sweatshop labor in developing Asian countries:* Their primary concern with profit maximization is—in the case of sweatshop labor— in conflict with the need to honor human rights such as those to fair and decent working conditions.

3. *People in developing Asian countries:* The need to satisfy the basic conditions for survival often motivates them to put up with exploitative treatment.

Our aim in examining the ethical challenges to US-Asia relations is to determine the best course of action for the first group in its exercise of political authority to address affronts to the third group's human rights, in relation to the second group's profit-motivated activities. We must consider that most in the third group would prefer the meager benefits that accrue from toiling in sweatshops to the grim alternative of being without this means of subsistence which could, in many cases, consequently lead to starvation and death. Despite the 'string of tragedies'—the latest of which involved the collapse of the Rana Plaza factory building and 190 deaths on 24 April—Bangladesh's garment industry is still thriving. Workers there were paid as little as $37 a month, but Bangladesh's garment manufacturing sector generated US$20 billion in exports in 2012 for the impoverished country. The practical problem revolves around the fact that sweatshops are mutually beneficial, making both employees and workers better off, *even if the latter is not as much better off as critics think they ought to be*, thereby making it more difficult to give force to the normative arguments against sweatshops.

Moral Decision-Making in the Contemporary Environment

The intuitive objection to sweatshops is based on notions of dessert; clearly, sweatshop laborers deserve better working conditions, and it is unfair where they are deprived of just compensation for their labor. John Rawls' argument from the veil of ignorance would suggest that it cannot be fair for sweatshop workers to suffer under such appalling working conditions, precisely because even the very corporate business owners who fuel the demand for sweatshop labor cannot condone this from an objective and disinterested perspective. Considering the inequalities between the United States and developing Asian nations which have become more entrenched over the course of history, people in developing Asian countries are relatively worse off than those in the United States, with or without regulations against sweatshop labor. It therefore appears that sweatshop labor is an aspect of US-Asia relations that is symptomatic of a *systemic* disadvantaging of the latter. Rawls would suggest that in circumstances like these, the only morally acceptable course of action is one in which the net benefits accruing to the least-advantaged people of developing Asian countries is maximized. In practical terms, this means that US-Asia relations must pay special attention to these low-wage laborers and work toward better working conditions in production facilities so as to eventually eradicate their endemic exploitation.

On the other hand, the harsh realities of the existing economic environment suggest that the situation is more complicated. Despite the fact that workers in the developing world are in great *need* of help which sweatshops are well-positioned to provide, it cannot justify a *special* obligation on the part of business corporations or sweatshops to suffer a shift of burdens in the provision of higher wages, better working conditions, etc. If US companies had to incur greater production costs in this manner, there would be fewer economic initiatives for them to set up manufacturing facilities in developing Asian countries, which comparative advantage is low-wage labor. For instance, the Bangladeshi government, according to Scott Nova from the Worker Rights Consortium, understands that strict labor rights regulations would raise manufacturing costs and cause retailers to place orders elsewhere. The projected rise in minimum wage levels by up to 44% in Southeast Asia has left manufacturers in the region—who rely on hiring factory workers for less than US$200 a month—concerned about the possible exodus of investment that could dampen the region's continued competitiveness. Everyone suffers, but low-wage workers would be worst hit.

Companies are not charity organizations and are inevitably subjected to market mechanisms, but this does not mean that they can maximize their profits without regard for the well-being of sweatshop laborers. Immanuel Kant's practical moral imperative asserts that human beings must be treated as ends in themselves and not merely as a means, and so sweatshops are inherently unacceptable from a deontological perspective since their workers seem to be treated as mere instruments in the amassing of business profits. Yet, if sweatshop labor was simply banned, people in developing Asian countries who are critically reliant on these jobs for survival would suffer even more, and this is all the worse for their Kantian right to self-determination. This suggests that in the real world—or at least in this case—ideas of absolute right vs. wrong are at best inadequate, and cannot be conflated with ideas of better vs. worse, which account, more importantly, for the *relative outcomes* of decisions.

The Kantian right to self-determination has great intuitive force and cannot simply be abandoned. Yet, if deontology alone is an unsatisfactory approach to evaluating the moral value of sweatshop labor, perhaps the existing conditions of the modern economic world call for a supplementary utilitarian approach. Utilitarianism—defined by the likes of Jeremy Bentham and John Stuart Mill—considers how everyone's *collective* welfare may be maximized. Sweatshop workers are relatively better off than if they had no such work, as are the companies which benefit from lower production costs, and the governments of the United States and Asia, which further benefit from lucrative economic relations with each other. Normatively speaking, sweatshop labor is morally *wrong* and should be banned. Practically speaking, however, there are shades of gray representing better and worse outcomes of moral decision-making within the existing political and economic environment. Theoretically, the need to respect human rights is directly associated with deontology and not utilitarianism. Yet, the utilitarian relativization of outcomes appears—counter-intuitively—to support human rights in the case of sweatshop labor *better* than a strictly deontological approach which flatly denies that sweatshop labor could ever be morally acceptable.

US-Asia Relations and Sweatshops: The Normative Picture

Relations between the governments of the United States and Asia form the bedrock of their economic dealings, and are indispensable to addressing the ethical issues surrounding sweatshop labor. From a broader perspective, it seems that the biggest ethical challenge facing US-Asia relations is that of negotiating between different moral obligations amid circumstances which render them incompatibilities. The issue of sweatshop labor is an instance of how the governments of these nations are confronted with tradeoffs between the short and long-term as well as other different aspects of their people's interests. Developing Asian countries have a strong interest in attracting foreign investment from the United States in a bid to accelerate economic growth and transformation and have, in the past decade, begun liberalizing governmental policies. Yet, this also encourages sweatshop labor, and the governments of developing nations appear guilty of condoning human rights violations. Alternatively, banning sweatshops leaves all parties worse off, especially in the longer run and more critically impacting people in these developing Asian countries.

The broader ethical question is whether the US economy is progressing at the expense of their Asian counterparts, and what determines if this situation is morally acceptable. So far, this article has shown that given today's circumstances, sweatshop labor is at least morally ambiguous and at best permissible, especially if one is purportedly concerned about the interests of Asian sweatshop workers. Despite the fact that sweatshop workers are relatively better off with rather than without this means of employment, the fact remains that their present working conditions are affronts to human rights and can never under any circumstances be *encouraged*. Consequently, sweatshop labor—even in the current context—may be practically but never *normatively* permissible. This acute distinction between practical and normative perspectives can never be overlooked; ethical issues operate at both levels, while each may generate very different recommendations as in the case of sweatshop labor. Even while sweatshops are conceived in practical terms as the lesser of two evils, their moral value remains questionable at best.

Sweatshops must be eradicated, but not in isolation from the systemic conditions which gave rise to its pervasiveness in the first place. Meenakshi Ganguly from the Human Rights Watch suggests that consumers could help pressure retailers to bring about change. She cites the example of blood diamonds, where the industry was forced to change when consumers became more aware and avoided purchasing diamonds that were not properly sourced. The governments of the United States and Asian countries need to take active steps to eliminate the underlying causal factors supporting the demand for sweatshop labor without worsening the present condition of sweatshop workers. Besides raising awareness, they could work towards developing minimum wage regulations and labor laws, having these enforced on both sides, while simultaneously developing closer economic and political ties and additional economic incentives (besides low-wage labor) and infrastructure to continue attracting US companies to engage in mutually beneficial business partnerships. The materialization of positive developments could span decades, but these initiatives remain crucially important.

In conclusion, the controversy surrounding sweatshop labor is indicative of the ethical challenges facing US-Asia relations, highlighted by the need to negotiate incompatibilities between the relative costs and advantages that result from their interactions, and more broadly, between the practical and normative perspectives on such issues. What *must* be done is not always congruent with what *should* be done, although we cannot afford to lose sight of the latter. Human persons are the essential units that constitute and give meaning to nations and economies. Even as US-Asia relations aim at boosting overall economic progress, these countries cannot overlook the moral obligation of respecting and defending fundamental human rights, and must continuously work at reconciling these divergent concerns.

Does Cultural Globalization Positively Impact Communities?

Free Trade Enables a Greater Intermingling of Cultures

Radley Balko

Radley Balko is an award-winning journalist who writes for the Washington Post. He was a recipient of the Bastiat Prize for Journalism in 2017.

Anyone from a small town knows about the "Wal-Mart effect." The superstore—or a similar mega-retailer, such as Home Depot or Lowe's—moves into a community and, within a few years, mom-and-pop hardware stores, toy stores and other main street retailers are put out of business. Whether that's a good or bad thing is up for debate.

Some argue that the smaller stores go under because Wal-Mart offers a bigger selection of goods at low prices. Consumers benefit because they can do all of their shopping at one place, and save money in the process. Detractors say consumers get less choice, and that because stores like Wal-Mart are national chains, they buy goods at a national level, and so local producers of goods suffer too, and soon entire communities lose their identity to mega corporations. We've become a "Gap nation," they say.

Opponents of globalization fear that the Wal-Mart effect is taking place on a global level, too. They cringe when a McDonald's franchise opens up in the historic heart of Prague, or when public spaces in Latin America, China or Africa become littered with billboards and advertisements for Coca-Cola, Nike and Calvin Klein.

Globalization's advocates say that free trade and free markets don't dilute or pollute other cultures, they enhance them. Trade creates wealth, they say. Wealth frees the world's poorest people from the daily struggle for survival, and allows them to embrace,

"Globalization & Culture," by Radley Balko, Global Policy Forum, April 2003. Reprinted by permission.

celebrate and share the art, music, crafts and literature that might otherwise have been sacrificed to poverty. So who's right? Is globalization killing non-western cultures, or is it augmenting and enhancing them?

Who Shot J.R.?

The idea that American culture is encroaching on the rest of the world is not a new one. Richard Pells writes in *The Chronicle of Higher Education* that, as early as 1901, Briton William Stead published a book with the foreboding title *The Americanization of the World*. The 1904 World's Fair in St. Louis, MO was billed as a celebration of the 100th anniversary of the Louisiana Purchase. The fair ignited overseas anti-American backlash, however, when exhibits instead tended to celebrate an alleged American cultural, political, and even ethnic supremacy.

More recently, fears that American culture might usurp the rest of the world could be traced to the Marxist social critic Herbert I. Schiller. Schiller's breakthrough book, *Communication and Cultural Domination*, was published in 1976, and was a critique of the post World War II influx and influence of American corporation across international borders. In the mid-1980s, the debate again heated up when the dramatic series Dallas gained enormous popularity outside the United States. The show's mass appeal seemed to validate many of Schiller's theories, and sparked "cultural preservation" movements in Europe.

But as Ph.D. candidate Christopher Hunter points out in a paper presented to the International Institute of Communications, more recent studies have shown that the worldwide appeal of Dallas may have been more the result of the show's ability to draw on the unique characteristics of disparate cultures than a "lowest common denominator" appeal that effectively "dumbed down" cultures the world over. Hunter writes:

> A number of ethnographic studies showed that foreign cultures "read" the show in vastly different ways. Ien Ang (1985) found that Dutch women interpreted the program through their own

feminist agenda in opposition to the supposedly embedded message of patriarchy. Eric Michaels (1988) showed how Australian Aboriginals reinterpreted Dallas through their notions of kinship in a way quite contrary to the show's intended meaning. Finally, Liebes and Katz (1990) found very different cultural interpretations of the show among Arab, Jewish, American, and Russian viewers. Further, Liebes and Katz point out that Dallas failed miserably in Japan and Brazil, a seemingly unexplainable event given the supposedly overwhelming power of US content to bowl over other cultures.

Pell's *Chronicle of Higher Education* essay makes a similar point: that where US culture has been successful in generating transnational appeal, it's perhaps the result of America's own diverse, immigrant population, which is able to produce entertainment, products and services that naturally appeal to a wide array of tastes and demand. Pell suggests that's something to be celebrated, not admonished. "In the end, American mass culture has not transformed the world into a replica of the United States," Pell writes. "Instead, America's dependence on foreign cultures has made the United States a replica of the world."

McWorld

Perhaps the most influential essay on the west's "cultural imperialism" in the last twenty years was written by Benjamin Barber in a 1992 issue of the *Atlantic Monthly*. Entitled "Jihad vs. McWorld," Barber's article argued that most of the third world was either being commercialized by the west, or was being won over by radical Islam. Neither scenario, Barber wrote, was conducive to democracy or to development. "McWorld" became a catchphrase for the ubiquity of American corporations overseas, and Barber later wrote a book by the same name.

Conventional wisdom suggests Barber is right, and that there is an increasing anti-McWorld backlash in the developing world. Wherever there's anti-American sentiment, it seems, a McDonald's inevitably gets vandalized. When US forces began bombing campaigns in Kosovo and Afghanistan, McDonald's franchises in those regions were the targets of protests.

But other suggest that highly publicized attacks on American corporate franchises might be anomalous. Dr. James L. Watson edited a book entitled *Golden Arches East*, which looks at how the establishment of McDonald's franchises has affected communities in Asia. Dr. Watson believes the anti-McDonald's fervor exists among just a few upper-class activists and academics, that the vitriol for American logos overseas is overstated in the media, and that most middle and lower-class communities are happy to have the added culinary option of a McDonald's or a Pizza Hut.

In most communities, in fact, the McDonald's has conformed to local culture, not not the other way around. The McDonald's corporation notes that most all of its overseas franchises are locally owned, and thus make efforts to buy from local communities. McDonald's also regularly alters its regional menus to conform to local tastes. McDonald's in Egypt, for example, serve a McFelafel. Japan McDonald's serve "seaweed burgers." Indian McDonalds' don't serve beef at all. And some French McDonalds' serve rabbit.

Watson points out that in the countries he's studied, McDonald's has been "Asianized" more than Asia has been "supersized." Michael Chan is the chairman of a group of Hong Kong fast food restaurants called "Café de' Coral." In an interview with Radio Netherlands, Chan said the introduction of McDonald's and its unique methods of distribution and labor management provided a template for other, indigenous restaurants in the country to flourish.

Logos—"No" or "Pro?"

Another important voice in the globalization vs. local culture debate is that of Naomi Klein. Klein's book *No Logo* has become the anti-globlization primer for activists all over the world. It was described by the *New York Times* as "the anti-globalization movement's Bible." Klein's book posits that logos and corporate trademarks have become a kind of international language, and that their omnipresence in the third world has robbed many peoples of the chance to develop a distinctive culture. She laments the ever-shrinking supply of "unmarked public spaces," and argues that corporations today spend far too much time branding and expend far too little resources on, for example, poor labor conditions, or on bettering the communities where they've exported their manufacturing plants.

But a recent study by a communications expert at the University of Buffalo suggests that, at least when it comes to the Internet, western cultural influence is waning, not expanding. George A. Barnett says that despite its centralization and apparent domination by the west, the Internet has given distinct "civilization clusters" a vehicle to communicate more effectively and promote their respective interests. Other communication experts have also suggested that emerging media (the Internet, and satellite television, for example) might serve as a megaphone for voices from smaller economies. The Arab-language al-Jazeera television station is one example. Most experts also predict that Chinese will surpass English as the Internet's predominant language in just a few years.

There are other signs that western "cultural hegemony" might be a bit overstated, too. For example, European anti-globalization activists have long criticized Hollywood and its big-budget studios for monopolizing the world movie industry and, consequently, polluting other cultures with American iconolatry.

But according to a worldwide 1999 BBC poll, the most famous movie star in the world isn't Ben Affleck or Julia Roberts, but Amitabh Bachchan, an Indian film star probably unfamiliar to most Americans. Last January, the *New York Times* reported that even American television programming has begun to lose its appeal overseas. Reason magazine writer Charles Paul Freund notes that as of 2001, more than 70% of the most popular television shows in 60 different countries were locally produced. And an article in the British newspaper *The Guardian* last year points out that the top-grossing movies for 2002 in Japan, Germany, Spain, France and India weren't US imports, but were produced domestically.

The story is the same across the arts—movies, television, and literature—American pop culture exports may be well-known overseas, but as emerging economies develop, consumers naturally prefer entertainment produced by artists with whom they share common experiences. In his book *Creative Destruction*, economist Tyler Cowen also explains how music—perhaps the most accessible and identifiable sphere of a given peoples' cultural heritage—is almost always the result of cross-cultural influences.

Cowan writes that Trinidad's steel band ensembles, for example, "acquired their instruments—fifty-gallon oil drums—from the multinational oil companies." Cowen also points out that all of the Third World's musical hubs—Rio, Lagos, Cairo, etc.—"are heterogeneous and cosmopolitan cities that welcomed new ideas and new technologies from abroad." Even raggae, perhaps the most renowned musical genre associated with a particular culture, was the result of cultural trade and influence. Cowen writes that raggae emerged when migrant Jamaican sugar workers traveled to the American south and brought back with them a jones for African-American rhythm and blues. Raggae developed over the 1950's as Jamaicans picked up radio broadcasts from New Orleans and Miami. And yet for all of this western influence, Cowan still finds that developing countries still hunger most for music made at home. In India, domestically produced music makes up 96% of the market; in Egypt, 81%; in Brazil, 73%.

Wealth and Culture

Globalization's advocates argue that wealth invigorates culture, and that trade and access to international markets are the best way to create wealth. They point out that the Internet, for example, has given developing peoples all over the world a low-cost way of bringing crafts, textiles, and art to western consumers. In his book In *Defence of Global Capitalism*, Swedish author Johan Norberg argues that because of emerging technology, developing countries that quickly embrace borderless trade can make the leap to western world living standards in a fraction of the time it once took. "Development which took Sweden 80 years to accomplish," Norberg writes, "has been successfully reiterated by Taiwan in 25." As an example, Norberg cites an anecdote from the World Bank:

> Halima Khatuun is an illiterate woman in a Bangladeshi village. She sells eggs to a dealer who comes by at regular intervals. She used to be compelled to sell at the price he proposed, because she did not have access to other buyers. But once, when he came and offered 12 taka for four eggs, she kept him waiting while she used the mobile phone to find out the market price in another village. Because the price there was 14 taka, she was able to go back and get 13 from the dealer. Market information saved her from being cheated.

Norberg notes similar cases across the world, where villages in developing countries have pooled resources for mobile phone services, or Internet access, always with similar results. The Internet in particular is fast becoming the most effective way for developing peoples to get their goods to market quickly, avoiding many of the usual overhead costs of maintaining a business. It's also a convenient way around trade barriers and tariffs. Consequently, websites promoting African, Latin America and indigenous American goods are popping up all over the Web.

The wealth from access to markets, then, enables developing people to make the shift from sustenance economies to merchant economies, a transition that enables art and culture to flourish. There's little time for culture, globalization advocates point out, when you're scrambling for survival.

The late economist Peter Bauer spent most of his life studying how trade can move developing economies from poverty to prosperity. Bauer recognized in the mid-20th century that those developing countries with significant contact with western markets were also the countries showing the most economic promise and growth.

In his book *From Subsistence to Exchange*, Bauer wrote, "Contacts through traders and trade are prime agents in the spread of new ideas, modes of behavior, and methods of production.

External commercial contacts often first suggest the very possibility of change, including economic improvement." What's more, free traders point out that many times the merging of western and developing cultures often infuses new life and creativity into generations-old customs and traditions.

In addition to music, Cowen cites in his book several other examples in his book of great artistry from indigenous peoples that, in fact, was largely inspired by cross-cultural trade. Cowen cites the famed soapstone sculptures of the Canadian Inuit, which, Cowen writes "weren't practiced on a large scale until after World War II," when the practice was introduced to them by western artist James Houston. Cowen writes:

> Analogous stories are found around the world. The metal knife proved a boon to many Third World sculpting and carving traditions, including the totem poles of the Pacific Northwest and of Papua New Guinea. Acrylic and oil paints spread only with Western contact. South African Ndebele art uses beads that are not indigenous to Africa, but rather were imported from Czecholslovakia in the early nineteenth century. Mirrors, coral, cotton cloth, and paper—all central materials for "traditional" African arts—came from contact with Europeans. Cowen and like-minded globalists believe, then, that far from stifling indigenous culture, free trade has exposed it to new influences, and opened it to new avenues of creative exploration.

Where To From Here?

Opponents of globalization argue that the playing field isn't level. Free trade naturally favors larger economies, they say, and so the predominant western influence stifles the cultures and traditions of the developing world. Free traders argue that globalization enhances culture, and that, in any event, culture can't thrive in poverty. Both sides generally agree that subsidies, tariffs and other protectionist policies by developed countries against goods commonly produced in the third world (textiles, for example) hamper both culture and economic growth there.

With the onset of the Internet, satellite technology, cable television, and cellular and wireless networks, the biggest traditional barrier to global trade—distance—isn't much of a problem anymore. The Internet also makes import tariffs, another traditional barrier, more difficult to enforce.

One thing is certain: as we move forward, transnational trade will only become more frequent, and will continue to find new participants in new corners of the globe. And activists on both sides will continue to debate whether or not the intermingling of cultures and influences that will inevitably accompany the growing global marketplace is a good or bad thing for both the developed and developing world.

Culture Is Dynamic and Borrows from Other Cultures to Its Benefit

Stephan Magu

Stephan Magu is a professor in the department of history and political science at Hampton University.

H ow do we define cultural studies? Cultural studies scholars struggle with a succinct and inclusive definition of cultural studies. This research recognizes the breadth, depth, extent and importance of these enduring questions. However, it adopts Stuart Hall's (1986) definition of cultural studies as a mix of "the sum of the available descriptions through which societies make sense of and reflect their common experiences." It also view's cultural studies through Hall's (1990) anthropological dimension of social practices which translate into "a whole way of life" of a people.

Sperber and Claidiere's (2008) definition of culture leverages that of Richerson and Boyd, as "information capable of affecting individuals' behavior that they acquire from other members of their species through teaching, imitation, and other forms of social transmission." In their discussion, Boyd and Richerson allude to this view of culture as a dynamic process, holding that culture has inherited properties, including beliefs, values and attitudes, and the transmission of culture/cultural values through social interactions much as one might inherit genetic properties but with ability to choose behaviors thus evolving "divergences" and differences.

Bidney (1944) defines culture anthropologically as "acquired capabilities, habits or customs; and that culture is a quality or attribute of human social behavior and has no independent existence of its own." This notion of the dependence of culture on some form of medium for it to exist is important; Bidney adds that "human culture is acquired or created by man as a member of society and that it is communicated largely by language." I shall revisit these notions of culture, in my discussion of the adaptive nature of culture and cultural teachings with regard to communication.

Sztompka (1996) defines cultural processes as designed to "embrace the soft tissue of society, the intangible assumptions, premises, understandings, rules, and values." Johnson defines culture as processes, values, beliefs; as the sum of human experience within certain settings, and the intersections of production in a Marxist sense. This definition encompasses culture as a sum of the social and cultural conditions of production of especially capitalist commodities and their consumption and how their principles create power differentials in societal relations.

Cultural studies is not merely residual, post-modern "Marxist critical theory" but a collection of theories and ideas inclusive of Marxist critiques and other modern theoretical trends, such as constructivist and post-structuralist. Conceptualizing cultural studies hinges not only on the pedagogy and study of culture but also on the definition of culture. And while theories explaining cultural studies are not concise, its study has certain, well-established parameters, empiricism, methodology and other scientific attributes (rigor) present in other arts and sciences. For example, Sperber and Claidiere (2008) advance the view that that "cultural anthropology gets by without any clear and agreed upon definition of culture."

It is quite evident that the definitions and conceptualizations of cultural studies, whether a Marxist critical theory the influences of structuralist, post-structuralist or feminist critiques and definitions, is quite a contested notion. There is a clear fluidity and permeability of culture, cultural traditions, literature and other texts, through human interactions, communication, economic, social, political and other processes further accelerated by globalization, which is sometimes defined as globalization.

These interactions have produced structures of interdependence and interconnectedness. Interdependence occurs where one *geographical* part of society, irrespective of their cultural, economic or social structures, depends on technology, products, knowledge and other services from other *geographical* locations.

Culture and Communication: Globalizing Culture?

Culture is not static. It is constantly changing, or more precisely, *agents of culture, i.e.*, human beings, are always interacting with other agents. These interactions have temporal or permanent effects on both the "originators" and the "targets" of such contacts. They are facilitated by different processes, which over time have varied from economic to social, political, and religious reasons, facilitated by transport, communication and underwritten by technology. Globalization accelerates cultures' interactions and facilitates transmission of values from one group to another.

Globalization is defined as "the widening, deepening and speeding up of worldwide interconnectedness in all aspects of contemporary social life, from cultural to the criminal, the financial to the spiritual," and in the recent past, has rapidly accelerated. There are historic and contemporary aspects to globalization, especially as a "growing engagement between the world's major civilizations" as defined by Modelski. Three main schools of thought are associated with globalization: the hyperglobalizers, the skeptics and the transformationalists. The transformationalist school is persuasive: globalization, even from its multiple definitions, is creating transnational, multiple, and simultaneous group identities and memberships that exhibit characteristics of globalization. Simultaneously, these identities transcend geography—their geography is global—while they are unbound by time and space.

How is globalization seen as affecting nationality, culture and identity? Tomlinson suggests that "globalization lies at the heart of modern culture; cultural practices lie at the heart of globalization." This conceptualization risks defining culture and globalization in associational, parallel terms. Culture exists within specific groups before the densening of social, political and economic interconnections, but the two-way effects are clearly identifiable.

Debates on the exact nature and effects of cultural globalization show wide variance. Some view cultural globalization in terms of "the homogenization of the world under the auspices of American popular culture or Western consumerism in general." This implies that cultures are not discerning/selective. Neither are they seen as capable of surviving the onslaught of Western/American consumerism to adapt only those features and products that are compatible with the cultures, or those that propagate the course of such cultures. While there is a significant global influence of Americanism/Western consumerism, it is not always adopted *in toto* by the target cultures. The transformationalists, on the other hand, "describe the intermingling of cultures and peoples as generating cultural hybrids and new global cultural networks."

Held & McGrew (1999) suggest a(n) "absence of a systematic framework for describing cultural flows across and between societies." Pieterse (1999) disagrees, conceptualizing globalization as a multi-level, multi-disciplinary occurrence with different definitions, depending on the pedagogical area. For example, Pieterse suggests that in economics, economic internalization, globalizing production and global finance characterize globalization. For international relations, increasing interstate relations and progression of global politics are evident. For cultural studies, global communications and worldwide cultural standardization—Coca-Colonization and McDonaldization are primary indicators of globalization. This approach views globalization in multi-dimensional terms, rather than as one unitary process with net effects and outcomes wherever it is encountered. Indeed, Featherstone (1990) argues that "there may be emerging sets of 'third cultures,' which themselves are conduits for all sorts of diverse cultural flows."

Third, cultures embrace and aggregate the most critical, utilitarian elements of global cultures, especially those connected with technologically driven processes—transport and communication. And contrary to Stuart Hall's characterization of *encoder-message-decoder*, in the process of communication within a globalized culture, an individual negotiates a "third, hybrid identity" by utilizing features of all the collective identity and group memberships that they have acquired through socio-political, economic and socio-cultural processes e.g., migration, emigration, education.

Conceptual Framework

This research applies three primary theoretical approaches; the ultimate goal is to show culture as dynamic and adaptive processes even in the face of sustained interaction with foreign cultures. These approaches include Arjun Appadurai's modernity at large, the hybridity approach and the notion of complex connectivity. These approaches generally demonstrate that cultures are not static; indeed, they are quite dynamic. The dynamism of cultures allows them to adopt (sometimes) the best attributes of other cultures and transform them into utilitarian objects to sustain or further the culture in question. Despite using the same vignettes that transmit cultures—television or movies—cultures adopt these (technologies) rapidly and, thus, it is not necessarily the case that cultural heterogenization occurs.

Appadurai, in his 1996 seminal work, *Modernity At Large: Cultural Dimensions of Globalization* argues that "the central problem of today's global interactions is the tension between cultural homogenization and cultural heterogenization. A vast array of empirical facts could be brought to bear on the side of the homogenization argument." In acknowledging the reasoning behind homogenization but contradicting its main argument, Appadurai show the dynamism of culture and the integration of the new cultural attributes into existing culture. "As rapidly as these forces from various metropolises are brought into new societies, they tend to become indigenized on one another way: this is true of music and housing styles as much as it is true of science and terrorism, spectacles and constitutions."

Appadurai goes on to propose "an elementary framework for exploring" the "certain fundamental disjunctures between economy, culture and politics." These "five dimensions of global cultural flows can be termed as (a) *ethnoscapes*; (b) *mediascapes*; (c) *technoscapes*; (d) *financescapes*; and (e) *ideoscapes*" that exhibit "fluid, irregular shapes". Appadurai adds that "these are not objectively given relations that look the same from every angle of vision, but rather, that they are deeply perspectival constructs, influenced by the historical, linguistic and political situatedness of different sorts of actors." Hickey-Moody adds that "exchanges between ethnoscapes, mediascapes, and ideoscapes are closely related and offer a way through which we can see the everyday life experiences."

It is important to pay attention to the contra-argument of cultural imperialism—one that, Gordon recounts as suggesting a concern among the developing countries "over what was perceived to be a one way flow of information and cultural goods from North to South or from East to West." A further argument was that these countries' "cultural sovereignty was being undermined by an unfair dominance that more industrialized countries wielded on the international communication scene." However, this view glosses over the fact that most of the developing countries were not homogeneous to begin with; in fact, as Appadurai observes, there were fears of cultural indigenization from majority groups within the nation more than there were fears of Americanization/ Westernization.

The second theoretical approach is "hybridity", proposed by Marwan Kraidy (2005). Kraidy describes hybridity in terms of capturing "the spirit of our times with its obligatory celebration of cultural difference and fusion." Acknowledging the growing and pervasive use of and description of "multipurpose electronic gadgets, designer agricultural seeds, environment-friendly cars with dual combustion and electrical engines, companies that blend American and Japanese management practices, multiracial people, dual citizens and postcolonial cultures," Kraidy uses hybridity to refer "mostly to culture but retains residual meanings related to the three interconnected realms of race, language, and ethnicity."

Kraidy adds that "since hybridity involves the fusion of two hitherto relatively distinct forms, styles or identities, cross-cultural contact, which often occurs across national borders as well as across cultural boundaries, is a requisite for hybridity." Globalization, which accelerates cultural contacts between individuals, groups and nations, therefore, particularly through communication, provides the interactional forum to facilitate fusion and/or creation of hybrid cultures. Burke writes of Edward Said's view of hybridity, in that "all cultures are involved in one another, none is single and pure, all are hybrid, heterogeneous." One might add that over time, and over their interactions, cultures have been borrowing from each other dynamically.

The third framework for conceptualizing this debate is through the "cultural connectivity" lens. Tomlinson writes of proximity as "increasing global-spatial *proximity*" ('the annihilation of space by time'" (Marx) and "time-space compression." "Proximity has its own truth as a description of the condition of global modernity, and this is generally of either a phenomenological or a metaphorical order", writes Tomlinson. "In the first case, it describes a common conscious *appearance* of the world as more intimate, more compressed, more part of everyday reckoning—for example, in our experience of rapid transport or our mundane use of media technologies to bring distant images into our most intimate local spaces. In the second, it conveys the increasing immediacy and consequentiality of real distanciated relations." These are some of the concepts that are generally used to describe the processes and consequences of globalization (e.g., compression); one no longer needs to be in the same geographical space to hold meetings; these can be done remotely.

Tomlinson provides an example of "the transformation of spatial experience into temporal experience that is characteristic of airline journeys. Planes are truly time capsules. When we board them, we enter a self-contained and independent temporal regime."

Titley highlights another outcome of the complex connectivity developed by Tomlinson, writing that "the enduring essentialism of culture may actually be read as a reaction to the deterritorialization: a reassertion of belonging and legitimacy in the face of real perceived flows of people, finance, images and ideas."

Even as cultures interact with others and ultimately create hybrid cultures, they adapt and reinvent themselves in effect, resituating themselves and propagating a process of self-reinvention. Ultimately, Tomlinson equates globalization with complex connectivity, writing that "globalization refers to the rapidly developing and ever-densening network of interconnections and interdependencies that characterize modern social life" and further, that "the notion of connectivity is found in one form or another in most contemporary accounts of globalization." One might perhaps erroneously conclude that one is the other but one of the agents of hybridity—however, the vignettes of globalization—have an effect on culture but also contribute to its adaptation processes.

Individuals, Communities, and Consumption: Agency

Individuals' roles in the transmission of culture—even those participating in a globalized world—cannot be underestimated. Individual decisions and choices—*agency*—are critical to the processes of cultural globalization, wherever it is evident. McCracken argues that "cultural meaning flows continually between its several locations in the social world, aided by the collective and individual efforts of designers, producers, advertisers, and consumers." In this flow, the qualities and characteristics of the good, which reflect the origin, are transferred to the "new" individual user. The utilitarian nature of modern consumer products permeates across cultures. A television, for example, serves the same purpose in an occidental home as it would an oriental, even as the frequency, individual or communal nature of use/enjoyment potentially differs. Similarly, the availability of a consumer good expands individual choice and the need for "more" thereby facilitating the expansion of cultural exchanges.

This homogeneity of cultural experiences view (including production and consumption processes) aligns with Dicken's conception of living in a world "in which consumer tastes and cultures are homogenized and satisfied through the provision of standardized global products created by global corporations with no allegiance to place or community." An indispensable element of the cumulative effect here is individual choice and agency: that which an individual does out of "self-interest" has effects that surpass any anticipated consequences.

The "butterfly effect" is a concept used to illustrate the effects of one small action/decision as having system-wide effects. It has generally been used to demonstrate the interconnectedness of systems in such a way that when one part of the system suffers shock or disruption, including the introduction of chaos to the system, the other parts of the interconnected system are affected, as illustrated by Shinbrot, Ditto, Grebogi, Ott, Spano and Yorke (1992) in their work "using the sensitive dependence of chaos (the 'butterfly effect') to direct trajectories in an experimental chaotic system."

Similarly, in cultural studies, individual choices and actions, where individuals exercise rational choice and attempt to maximize their utility in light of their preferences and available choices, acquisition of merchandise or other cultural texts can have lasting changes to their local experiences and way of life. An important illustration of this concept can be found in the film, *The Gods Must Be Crazy*, a humorous example of changes that "foreign objects" can bring into the "normal" that a different community may have traffic with. Similarly, the Swahili language has had to "invent" words for "texts" such as TV (*runinga*), a computer (*kompyuta*), World Wide Web (*mtandao*)—words and concepts that did not exist prior to the invention of the "texts" to which they refer.

Communication and Technology: The Mainstays of Globalized Culture

For any cultural process to transcend geographical limits and spaces, transport and communication has been instrumental in facilitating their spread. The history of transportation (either by human, animal or motorized/mechanized means) has grown hand-in-hand with the history of trade, industrialization and modernization. Indeed, cultural exchanges were facilitated by these processes, which often utilized language (sign, spoken, written) to communicate from one group to the other. Illustrious histories of the travels of Christopher Columbus, Amerigo Vespucci, Vasco da Gama, Henry Morton Stanley, Johann Ludwig Krapf, among others, adorn history books and therefore propagate certain cultural traditions and our conceptualization of the same, e.g., of adventure.

The process of transport and communication has been accelerated, over man's history, by producing better and faster inventions e.g., the invention of the wheel, chariots, ocean-going vessels, steam-ships, motor-cars, airplanes, the telephone, computers and Internet, among others. Indeed, as Vertovec writes on telecommunication, "international phone call volume rose from 12.7 billion call minutes in 1982, almost fourfold to 42.7 billion in 1992 and another fourfold to 154 billion by 2001" ([25], p. 219). Given this trajectory, it is reasonable to assume another fourfold increase to approximately 700 billion call minutes by 2010 will be achieved, and given the accelerating pace of globalization and communication explosion through cellular networks, satellite, fiber-optics and voice over Internet protocols (VoIP), the estimate may be well short of actual figures.

As Vertovec further postulates, "this obviously has considerable impact on domestic and community life, inter-generational and gender relations, religious and other cultural practices, and local economic development in both migrant sending and migrant-receiving contexts." During these communication processes, transmission of beliefs, ideas, thoughts, and practices occurs. Even where dilution of culture is not necessarily evident, the long-term effect may lead to not only adoption of "foreign" cultural traits, but to an assimilation of such traits. One of the most pertinent examples of this type of assimilation was practiced as a "national colonial policy" by France in Africa.

Case Studies: Communication— The Personal and the Global

The dominant paradigm in the construction of power relations (both in international relations, and in the global economy) has structured relations as a Global North and Global South binary, with clear differences. The historical account of the Renaissance in Europe, the conquest of "barbaric peoples" and their eventual civilization elevates the Global North's narrative and diminishes that of the Global South. The construction of communication processes is similar: the north is "developed" and the south is somewhat "primitive" (I am cognizant that the reproduction of these stereotypes only reinforces this binary). Perhaps a more accurate conception would be that of difference.

Given the different levels of development, examining literature on communication especially relating in Global South countries, which are recipients of technological, economic and ideological ideas from the north, and the targets of cultural "modernization/development/civilization" is useful. The perpetuation of this dependent relationship and differences is constantly disseminated through media: content, hardware, software, technical expertise, *etc.* The diffusion of cultural ideas is packaged in four approaches, including communication effects, mass media and modernization, diffusion of innovation and social marketing, all of which, combined, proliferate western ideas to the "south." This becomes one *method* for cultural transference, retention and transmission of attitudes, beliefs and other cultural aspects.

Often conversations around the use of cultural artifacts as socialization/cultural hegemony method have often underestimated the desirability of the very artifacts to the recipient communities. The existence and use of Global South artifacts and their usefulness and their impact on communities that *need* them is often taken for granted. Adorno and Horkheimer's discussion of cultural artifacts and the mechanical production of such objects, which leads to the loss of the aura (the artistic nature of the object), loses sight of the necessity of using the artifacts, pitted against the costs incurred of not adopting their uses, even at the expense of "diluting" culture.

The invention of the motor-car, for instance, may well have been an artistic venture by an individual. The aura of the car is not debatable, but it is difficult to argue that the mass-production of the car (as a "text") and its subsequent "transmission" to other cultures has not, on average, improved quality of life. Therefore, accepting the use of foreign cultural artifacts created either as artistic objects or for their utilitarian value, the cost associated with resisting new artifacts is often higher than the cost of adaptation to their uses.

Hall criticizes the traditional conception of (mass) communication as a process between sender/message/receiver and proposes a "complex structure of dominance" through which meaning and interpretation is formulated as communication is passed on from one source to another, through media, its meaning encoded and decoded, translated and transformed and given meaning, and *thus* "consumption" occurs. The *medium* of transmission of messages often follows the traditional sender/message/receiver variant, enabled by symbols and "texts" of mass communication.

[...]

Communication, Political Participation (Protest), and Color Revolutions

The proliferation of different communication methods and gadgets has made easier interpersonal communication and facilitated changes in political landscape. One of the earliest interactions between mobile communication and political actions was the 2004 Ukrainian "Orange Revolution." This revolution heralded not only popular "mass action" by social groups using social media to organize; it also showed the duality of limitation of government control and influence that communication has on personal attitudes and choices. In the Ukraine "Orange Revolution," Premier Yuschenko's supporters used both online (web) communication and mobile technology. Kuzio argues that, "the opposition made effective use of cell phones, during both the election campaign and the revolution itself. In a now-infamous video clip, recorded by an oppositionist's cell-phone camera, a university professor is seen illegally instructing his students to vote for Yanukovych."

Elections in other contexts have not always used technologies to organize, for example in the case of Kenya in 2008. In other instances, government purposely targets such communication avenues to frustrate mass organization and promote the pursuit of tyrannical rule, as discussed by Addis on the 2009 Iranian elections. Cohen writes of Iranian youth:

> It is not uncommon for them to send messages to one another by peer-to-peer Bluetooth messaging on their mobile phones. The Bluetooth technology enables young Iranians to send messages to anyone with a wireless feature on their mobile phones, even if they don't know either their name or telephone number.

This application of cultural artifacts derived of a global mindset (for, after all, the mobile phone is a "Western" cultural text) shows clearly that cultures and communities/groups (even oppressed ones, like the Iranian youth) innovate and apply the texts and technology availed through the processes of globalization expanded concepts of social, group and interpersonal communication.

Predicting Future Trends in Global Culture— *More Homogeneity or Heterogeneity?*

Will the future be more homogeneous or heterogeneous, especially regarding culture and identity? The question of whether the world is moving towards being more globalized/Americanized/Westernized remains a lightning rod. What is clear is that the processes of interconnectedness and greater cultural integration through travel, commerce, migration and recreation, have brought exposure to Western "freedoms", human rights, and capitalist democracy; these interactions affect both Western and non-Western societies, causing a hybrid, rather than distinct, pure cultures.

The growing interconnectedness between peoples, places and lifestyles (otherwise known as globalization) will require not only shifting production to other countries but increasing knowledge of distant cultures and peoples. In addition, the changing demographics due to immigration, travel, leisure or temporal interactions, will have an effect on the conception of identity and culture. Whether the notion of approximately 40% of the world's population being in two countries (India and China) influences cultures to be insular in an attempt to preserve their core values and identities, or whether the inevitability of greater integration leads to a more homogeneous world remains to be seen.

Conclusions

The world we live in is characterized by accelerating, intensifying and deepening social, economic, cultural, religious and recreational interconnections between one geographic and cultural area of one people to another. These interconnections have led to, and been characterized by, a respatialization and re-structuring of human relations occasioned and supported by rapid developments in technology, communication and language. The argument that Westernization/Americanization is impacting foreign cultures in a way that aims to change and heavily influence foreign cultures is shown to carry some weight, but cultures are also selective of processes they adapt.

Cultures often retain their unique features even as they borrow and adopt features of other cultures they interact with. The notion that American/Western culture overwhelms other cultures based on commerce and consumption models ignores the localization of the very structures and essences of the foreign culture (e.g., cell phone use in native languages, adoption of Swahili by the Google search engine, among others). Culture and society adopts technology and fashions it to meet its needs without necessarily fundamentally changing those cultures.

Traditionally, globalization is associated with Westernization/Americanization, but cultures are indeed dynamic, and are not simply victims of globalization and Westernization. They have adopted those "texts" that allow them to be competitive and adaptive of changes occurring within the local and global contexts. If communities and cultures did not adapt, many African countries would still be using runners and smoke signals to communicate, rather than radio signals and cell phones, and the Greeks would still have marathon runners even in times of battle.

Hall argues that technology and mass media/mass communication, one of the primary tools for globalization and culturally influencing other countries, propagates a specific agenda, usually constructed by the powerful and embedded in the message as well as the mode of transmission. However, the availability of those same technological devices has enabled cultures to adopt and customize technologies for local use, including their application through language and mass media. It is conceivable, however, that Hall's argument holds at the community, rather than the national level, where *elites* within the specific communities influence the construction of the message and further control the medium/media by which the constructed messages are delivered to the audiences.

On a global scale, cultures have increasingly utilized modern technology and other developments by adopting and integrating them with best practices, which enables inter-state communications in foreign languages, thereby supporting globalization on the one hand but also localizing and personalizing global texts (e.g., the cell phone) to local uses (e.g., communication in mother-tongues) and, further, applying these global texts to local situations both at the local and national levels (e.g., organizing the protests in Iran and Ukraine). The argument that the global becomes local, and the local becomes global holds. Globalization impacts local and global trade, commerce, leisure, entertainment, and other areas of human interaction and provides an enriching individual experience tempered and allows individuals to interact with the processes of globalization in a very personal way.

Cultural Exchange Does Not Mean a Nation's Loss of Identity

Abderrahman Hassi and Giovanna Storti

Abderrahman Hassi is affiliated with the School of Business Administration and Giovanna Storti with the Language Centre, both at the Al Akhawayn University, Morocco.

Transnational flows of people, financial resources, goods, information and culture have recently been increasing in a drastic way and have profoundly transformed the world (Ritzer and Malone, 2001). This phenomenon has been labeled globalization. As a result, a great deal of debate and discussion, even controversy (Bird and Stevens, 2003) has taken place about globalization in various disciplines from different angles. In fact, there seems to be a controversy in regards to globalization and the contradictory meanings associated with it. This controversy refers, among others, to either "a dominant logic of globalization" which postulates that there is a single cause for globalization or to a "phenomenon with a complex set of causes" which argues that there are various causes for globalization (Beck, 2000). In corollary, research has not been successful in grasping the globalization phenomenon in its entirety.

Globalization is a multidimensional phenomenon that encompasses not only economic components but also cultural, ideological, political and similar other facets (Prasad and Prasad, 2006). Consequently, globalization has been addressed from the points of view of economics, social sciences, politics and international relations and has been subject to endless debates in various disciplines. Nonetheless, globalization effects are rarely addressed as a determinant that impacts societies and their cultures. More precisely, the interaction between globalization and culture still remains under-researched (Prasad and Prasad, 2007) and the current globalization debate in this respect is relatively recent (Acosta and Gonzalez, 2010). Along the same lines, the literature has not been able to stress whether concepts such as Americanization and McDonaldization are synonymous with globalization (Latouche, 1996).

In an increasingly borderless world impacted by a globalization of economies, the preservation of cultural diversity feeds contrary and controversial reactions. For instance, Cowen (2002) contends that while changes and potential losses imposed by globalization on local and traditional cultures, including those extending to cultural differences, may be damaging and destructive, they may also lead towards new prospective opportunities.

Given the above context, it is argued that globalization brings about diverse trends, namely cultural differentiation, cultural convergence and cultural hybridization (Pieterse, 1996) and each trend does not preclude the other as cultural homogeneity and heterogeneity are complementary (Cowen, 2002).

[...]

Culture

Scholars and researchers do not agree on a general definition of culture with over 150 plausible definitions identified in the 1950s (Kroeber and Kluckholn, 1952). In fact, culture has been studied from various fields such as anthropology, sociology and psychology. Hofstede (1980:25) defines culture as "the collective programming of the mind which distinguishes the members of one group or society or category or nation from another." The '66mind' refers to thinking, feeling and acting, with consequences for beliefs, attitudes and behaviors. In this regard, values and systems of values constitute a core element of culture. While the concept of 'culture' can be applied to any human collectivity, it is often used in the case of societies which refer to nations, ethnic entities or regional groups within or across nations (Hofstede, 2001). As such, culture is concerned with a distinct environment of a community about which members share meaning and values (House et al., 1999). As for Kroeber and Kluckholn (1952: 181):

> *Culture consists of patterns, explicit and implicit, of and for behavior acquired and transmitted by symbols, constituting the distinctive achievement of human groups, including their embodiment in artifacts; the essential core of culture consists of traditional ideas and especially their attached values; culture systems may, on the one hand, be considered as products of action, on the other, as conditioning elements of future action.*

In addition, Bennett and Bennett (2004) distinguish between an objective culture, which refers to the institutional aspects of a culture and a subjective culture that focuses on a worldview of a society's people.

On another note, Cowen (2002) contends that culture refers to art products and activities, as well as, other creative products that stimulate and entertain individuals such as music, literature, visual arts and cinema. In this regard, some populations use their culture to create new products making culture a commercial label.

A worthwhile observation is the fact that culture is not rigid. It is a process that gradually builds up through interaction. Culture allows individuals to create human societies by defining the conditions of how people live among each other and together, as well as, by abiding to social and cultural codes that distinguish them from other cultures.

In a nutshell, the concept of culture has two major definitions. On the one hand, culture is an integrated set of values, norms and behaviors acquired by human beings as members of a society. As such, culture constitutes an element of identification within a given group of individuals and an element of differentiation vis-à-vis other groups from an anthropological standpoint. On the other hand, from a sociological stance, culture refers to artistic and symbolic creations, heritage and cultural products. In relation to globalization, these two aspects have important implications with respect to how individuals express their cultural identities, in terms of the future of cultural traditions, and with cultural industries. Therefore, for purposes of the present chapter, the concept of culture refers to the two above-mentioned aspects.

Globalization and Culture

For millions of years, human groups spanned over immense territories without means of communications other than reliance on their physical body parts such as their eyes, voices, hands and legs. With the advent of the urbanized metropolitan cities dating back to more than 5,000 years ago and the beginning of commercial activities, cultural exchanges have taken place between individuals living among various societies. However, in the past, means of communication and transportation were limited and cultural characteristics did not circulate as rapidly and easily as in modern times.

With the industrial revolutions, societies began to have access to machines which allowed them to create cultural products and export them across borders. By the 18th century, thinkers had forecasted a non-reversible trend of cultural standardization. However, the predominance of the nation-state and national economic barriers had protected and insulated cultures from external influence. Cultural uniformization based on the European model at the end of 18th century was prevalent, particularly due to the success of the rational capitalism that characterized Europe and which was the symbol of cultural modernity (Weber, 1905). Additionally, the enlightenment thinkers had forecasted a uniformized and borderless world in the sphere of values. In the 19th century, cultural industries depended on technical innovations during the first and second industrial revolutions such as, printing in 1860, and electricity and cinema in 1890. Further, cultural miscegenation-related fear dates back to 1853 when Arthur de Gobineau wrote an influential essay on the inequality of human races in France. Marx and Engels noted an intellectual convergence in the literature which was a kind of intellectual globalization of ideas that preceded the materialistic globalization of goods and markets. As for the German intellectual Goethe, he pleaded for a world culture through world literature (Weltlitertur) where everybody would contribute. In the 20th century, cultural industries appeared as communication technology started to develop and flow seaminglessly across borders.

[…]

Heterogenization Scenario

While certain scholars (i.e. Appadurai, 1996; Featherstone, 1995) admit that globalization for the most part originates from Western cultures, they however reject the idea that this phenomenon constitutes a homogenization of world cultures resulting from one way exchanges among the latter. In fact, this "school of thought" argues that globalization generates rather a state of heterogeneity which refers to a network structure in which nodes tend to connect with each other in regard to certain cultural dimensions (Matei, 2006). Two distinct variants of heterogenization can be distinguished (Chan, 2011). The heterogenization at a local level refers to a situation where the practices of a sphere of life in a specific milieu or locale become more diverse over a period of time. The heterogenization at a trans-local or global level refers to a situation where the practices of a sphere of life in at least two locales become more distinct over a period of time. In short, heterogenization, which has also been labeled differentiation, relates fundamentally to barriers that prevent flows that would contribute to making cultures look alike (Ritzer, 2010). In this perspective, cultures remain different one from another.

Heterogenization represents a process which leads to a more inwardly appearing world due to the intensification of flows across cultures (Appadurai, 1996). Hence, local cultures experience continuous transformation and reinvention due to the influence of global factors and forces. It is important to keep sight of the fact that according to this perspective, cultures do not remain unaffected by global flows and globalization in general, but the actual crux of the culture remains intact and unaffected, as has always been (Ritzer, 2010) with only peripheral surfaces directly impacted.

The convergence thesis advancing that globalization favors homogenization of the world underestimates the global flows of goods, ideas and individuals. In this regard, Robertson (2001), who is critical of the focus on processes stemming from the United States and its homogenizing impact on the world, advocates the notion of heterogeneity with a focus on diversity, multi-directional global flows and the existence of world processes that are independent and sovereign of other nation-states. These flows do not eradicate local cultures, they only change some of their traits and reinforce others. Along the same line, Wiley (2004) contends that national cultures, which are fluid constructs, have become part of a heterogeneous transnational field of culture.

Different cultural groups develop into heterogonous entities due to differences in demands necessitated by their environment in efforts to adapt to the requirements of the latter. And consequently over a period of time, these groups become diversified and very different due to environmental circumstances and pressures. For instance, although the spread of the colonization phenomena yielded a reduction of cultural differentiation, when the colonization movement receded, cultures sprung up and cultural differentiation was favored.

In sum, it has been documented in some instances that foreign cultural practices remain in the margins of local and national cultures resulting in a side-by-side coexistence of distinct and disparate global and local cultures (Prasad and Prasad, 2006). It seems that cultural differentiation will most likely remain strong despite globalization forces. What will probably change is the criteria used by different cultural groups to define their identity and differentiation vis-à-vis other cultures.

The Homogenization Scenario

Are international exchanges and flows of goods, services, capitals, technology transfer and human movements creating a more standardized and unique world culture? Would acculturation, which yields from long and rich contacts between societies of different cultures, result in a universal culture?

The homogenization perspective seems to positively answer these questions as the increased interconnection between countries and cultures contributes to forming a more homogenous world adopting the Western Euro-American model of social organization and life style (Liebes, 2003). In the homogenization view, barriers that prevent flows that would contribute to making cultures look alike are weak and global flows are strong (Ritzer, 2010). In its extreme form, homogenization, which is also known as convergence, advances the possibility that local cultures can be shaped by other more powerful cultures or even a global culture (Ritzer, 2010). This perspective is reflected in several concepts and models such as the Global Culture, Americanization and more importantly the McDonaldization theory.

Across different regions and countries in the world, more and more people seem to watch the same entertainment programs, listen to the same music, consume common global brand products and services, and wear the same or similar clothes (Prasad and Prasad, 2006).

These comparable developments in cultural practices are suggestive of the emergence of a "global culture" (Robertson, 1992) or "world culture" (Meyer, Boli, Thomas and Ramirez, 1997) based on the assumption of the demise of the nation-state as a major player on the global stage (Ritzer, 2010). In other terms, globalization contributes in creating a new and identifiable class of individuals who belong to an emergent global culture. According to this concept, the selfsame dynamics of globalization are weakening the connections between geographical places and cultural experiences (Held and McGrew, 2003), and eroding the feeling of spatial distance which tends to reinforce a sense of national separateness (Prasad and Prasad, 2006). Thus, globalization, which is a replication of the American and/or Western cultural tradition (Beck, 2000; Berger, 2002), is considered a destructive force, a recipe for cultural disaster (Jaja, 2010) and an assault on local cultures which the latter are not able to withstand or resist (Berger, 2002). This is presumably due to the fact that globalization contributes in atrophying identities and destroying local cultural traditions and practices, diluting, even eliminating the uniqueness of national cultures, and establishing a homogenized world culture.

However, some proponents of the concept of global culture argue that the latter is not cohesive in nature and refers to a set of cultural practices that only bear surface resemblance. Moreover, Smith (2003) completely rejects the existence of the notion of global culture whether as a cohesive or discordant concept. Along the same lines, Tomlinson (2003) maintains that globalization makes individuals aware of the diverse national cultures in the world which are multiple in numbers and distinct in nature. Hence, globalization strengthens national cultures rather than undermine them.

On another note, Jaja (2010) stresses that the world is presently experiencing Americanization, rather than globalization with the former referring to the global spread of America's influential dominance and culture through drastic growth of mass communication and penetration of American companies in other countries. As a matter of fact, there seems to be an American hegemony reflected by a domination of the Internet as 85% of web pages originate from the United States and American companies control 75% of the world's packaged software market (Jaja, 2010). In addition to the latter, there is an American monopoly of the media as seen with popular films, music, and satellite and television stations around the globe. It should be highlighted that the American conception of culture is open and far from the *erudite* notion of several European countries, for instance. Further, the American way of life does not appear to be elitist and aims at spreading cultural products to the masses which increase economic opportunities. This model is desired by other populations, developed and developing.

Nonetheless, it has been documented that only countries that share values similar to those of the United States are more inclined to adopt products which reflect the American culture and consider them as their own; conversely, cultures with values different than those of the United States are less likely to embrace products typical of the American culture (Craig, Douglas and Bennett, 2009). Therefore, the Americanization phenomena seems to be contingent with the predisposition of local cultures to embrace artifacts reflective of the American culture, rather than with the simple availability of these artifacts.

[…]

Conclusion

[…]

There is no doubt that cultures get influenced and shift through contact with other cultures. However, this influence and shift does not mean cultural standardization or convergence towards a world cultural model based on the American or the European one. Some authors have rejected the simplistic idea of homogenization and convergence (see Garrett, 1998) as there is empirical evidence that supports the fact that globalization preserves national particularities (Guillén, 2001; Zelizer, 1999). In fact, nations will maintain their variety and complexity, and cultural diversity is not endangered as cultural differences between countries are maintained. Nations get involved in cultural integration processes on a regular basis without loosing their cultural peculiarities. They interpret cultural elements in light of theirs in a way that they become compatible with their culture. The adoption of a Western way of life does not mean standardization. Human societies resort to their symbolic fences in order to express their particularity and difference as a set of customs, habits, practices and productions.

To benefit from opportunities, cultures do not shut themselves off from the rest of the world, but rather they open up to other cultures in efforts to improve their social and economic capabilities.

Culture openness is a phenomenon that recognizes differences between cultures, does not necessarily standardize or blend cultures and allows cultures to benefit from richness of other cultures. In the old days, individuals were subject to cultural consequences as they had to live with what their environment transmitted to them in addition to their contribution. Culture was part of individuals' destiny as it shaped their identity and future. Nowadays, individuals have access to an immense ocean of data and information which influence their socialization through acquired behaviors and attitudes. However, these acquired elements do not constitute a source of destruction to the core components of their own native culture.

[…]

The Global Spread of New Media Technologies Threatens Indigenous Cultures

Vineet Kaul

Vineet Kaul is affiliated with the department of communication and media in the Dhirubhai Ambani Institute of Information and Communication Technology in Gandhinagar, Gujarat, India.

In both scholarly work and public debate on globalization, the influence of media and particularly electronic media on social change is considered to be of paramount importance. In sociological and cultural analyses of globalization, media such as satellite television, the Internet, computers, mobile phones etc. are often thought to be among the primary forces behind current restructurations of social and cultural geography. Electronic media facilitate an increased interconnectedness across vast distances and a temporal flexibility in social interaction. Furthermore, development, imperialism and globalization are three ideas which have been designed to interpret and change the world. They can frequently be seen rubbing shoulders in discussions of international questions in the social sciences but what they mean to each other is often anything but clear. The concept of globalization is one of the most debated issues since the collapse of communism. Most discourse on globalization acknowledges that it is an 'uneven' process. Its effects and consequences are not uniformly experienced everywhere in the world and there is a 'power geometry' of globalization in which 'some people are more in charge of than others; some initiate flows and movement, other's don't; some are more on the receiving-end of it than others; some are effectively imprisoned by it and there is going to be an imbalance of power when dealing with two nations. The rapid acceleration

"Globalisation and Media," by Vineet Kaul, OMICS International, December 23, 2011. https://www.omicsonline.org/open-access/globalisation-and-media-2165-7912.1000105. php?aid=3360.

of globalization has for long been associated with technological advancement and the international market. On the one hand there is the tendency towards homogeneity, synchronization, integration, unity and universalism. On the other hand, there is the propensity for localization, heterogeneity, differentiation, diversity and particularism detrimental to development. These processes are intricately interwoven and represent—in reality—two faces of the same coin. Thus the term "globalizations" is sometimes used to indicate that globalization is not an ubiquitous or uniform process, but involves various terrains, manifests differently in various contexts and has different effects for people in different contexts.

The modern epoch opened as an era of globalization. Most of the critics portray this term as a world with permeable borders. The concept of globalisation is global and dominant in the world and it was not handed down from heaven, it was not decreed by the Pope, it did not emerge spontaneously. It was created by the dominant social forces in the world today to serve their specific interests. Simultaneously these social forces gave themselves a new ideological name the—"international community"—to go with the idea of globalisation (Madunagu 1999). The critics argue that today's globalisation is only superficially different from the old fashioned colonialism. Resistance to globalization is also not new; China has been resisting globalization since the Opium War in which Britain arm-twisted the Middle Kingdom for the right to sell Indian opium in the mainland. How is this any different from US pressure on Beijing on WTO? The British saw India as a source of raw materials for the empire, and a market for cotton. Today India is a source of cheap labor in the sweatshops of the information technology industry, and a huge market for consumer goods. Globalization is just imperialism in disguise, it has the same motive: control over resources and the right of might.

Some "anti-globalization" groups argue that globalization is necessarily imperialistic, is one of the driving reasons behind the Iraq war and is forcing savings to flow into the United States rather than developing nations; it can therefore be said that "globalization" is another term for a form of Americanization, as it is believed by some observers that the United States could be one of the few countries (if not the only one) to truly profit from globalization.

We see globalization as the extension of trends and influences (such as ideas, concepts, knowledge, ethics and technology as well as behaviors) across erstwhile barriers (ethnic, linguistic, cultural, religious, political or environmental). It must be emphasized that globalization is not merely a homogenizing and integrating force but it is also blamed for problems plaguing nations and individuals. We see that the global environment is being threatened on a number of fronts, from global warming and the deterioration of the ozone layer to the extermination of species and the poisoning of the world's water supply. Other economic consequences as a result of globalisation are the loss of jobs to developing countries such as China and India, where labour costs are cheaper. A lot of American and British based countries opt to have their products manufactured abroad to save money and hence increase profits. The globalisation of the world is stimulating massive amounts of investment by the transnational corporations which are "acting like a dynamo to produce more jobs and higher profits world wide." Often workers rights are not agreed and working conditions of those in developing countries manufacturing work out sourced by that of developed countries is poor. Everyday life has been Disneyfied, McDonaldized and Coca-Colonized (see Ritzer, 2004 and Barber, 1996). The iconography associated with global brands such as Microsoft, McDonald's, Nike or Pizza Hut transcends both space and language. Branded goods are manufactured in the far-east in 'sweat shops' where employees work for very low wages. Millions of people are unable to sustain their families since jobs are often moved from country to country by large trans national organisations so therefore employees are often only employed on a temporary basis, money therefore flows from one country to the next as factories and jobs are transferred from one to country to the next, with investment being given and taken away. Many of us have a gut feeling that the global economy has gone awry essentially calling for wholesale murder and maiming of innocent populace.

Global media systems have been considered a form of cultural imperialism. Cultural imperialism takes place when a country dominates others through its media exports, including advertising messages, films, and television and radio programming. America's dominance in the entertainment industries made it difficult for other cultures to produce and distribute their own cultural products. Supporters of American popular culture argue that the universal popularity of American media products promotes a global media system that allows communication to cross national boundaries. American popular culture in addition challenges authority and outmoded traditions. Critics of American culture contend that cultural imperialism prevents the development of native cultures and has a negative impact on teenagers. There has been much debate in international fora, in academia and among media professionals over the question of the potential threat to indigenous culture by the unprecedented global penetration of the new media technologies resulting from the enormous capacities for information access, transmission and retrieval, referred to by Rex Nettleford as "the hijacking of the region's media, the invasion of the people's intellectual space and the cultural bombardment of the entire region by every means possible from North America...." In the past decades, international aspects of mass media were being discussed by scholars and intellectuals under the auspices of UNESCO. Today, the media has transformed into a business that is dominated by mass-media corporations promoting their own interests at the level of individual administrations. In both scholarly work and public debate on globalization, the influence of media and particularly electronic media on social change is considered to be of paramount importance. In sociological and cultural analyses of globalization, media such as satellite television, the Internet, computers, mobile phones etc. are often thought to be among the primary forces behind current restructurations of social and cultural geography. Electronic media facilitate an increased interconnectedness across vast distances and a temporal flexibility in social interaction. Furthermore, a handful of media enterprises and media moguls such as Time-Warner-AOL, Disney, Rupert Murdoch, and Bill Gates have become icons of globalization. These media companies and actors both have ambitions of global market domination and serve as the messengers of a new global era. Particularly the transnational news services with a global or regional reach, such as CNN, BBC World, Euronews, Sky News, and Star News, have come to be regarded as the town criers of the global village. Their continuous, on-line, and live distribution of news to all corners of the world has become emblematic of a world in which place and time mean less and less.

[...]

Cultural Diversity

It is believed that commercialisation and an oligopolised media structure are definitely a threat to diversity and sovereignty of any nation. The porosity of cultural boundaries engendered by media globalization has given rise to concerns over cultural sovereignty and cultural rights. While such concerns have been dismissed by proponents of globalization as unfounded, for developing countries, the economic reality of which preclude the development of strong local productions and so foster reliance on imported programming, these concerns are quite relevant. Research has shown that where local productions are weak, inroads made by foreign media can be dangerous. Media privatization exacerbates this reliance and encourages the inflow of imported content on the principle that within a free market system, there should be no barriers erected against the free flow of cultural products across borders. Most importantly, as private media rely heavily on advertising money for economic viability, there is a constant stream of cultural goods that inundate the local scene by way of paid television commercials. These cultural products are rife with images reflecting cultural values and expectations concordant with the countries of origin and are at odds with the cultural and economical realities of receiving countries.

The media have become the chief transmitters of culture. The traditional showcases of culture—museums, theatres, art galleries or libraries—have handed over part of their functions to the cinema screens, television or computers; media where culture has greater distribution and scope, since the images reach broader, more heterogeneous and widespread audiences. Cultural diversity is recognized externally and internally, both by the prevailing institutions of civil society and by the awareness of the group itself as different to the whole in some expressions. The preservation of this diversity is one of the challenges with the homogenizing risk of a globalized world, where uniform cultural patterns are present. The following measures should be adopted in defense of cultural diversity:

- The political-social context itself, which plainly requires recognition on the part of cultural minorities, recommends the adoption of measures favouring and facilitating the expression of the different social groups through the media.
- The rapid expansion of the new technologies, especially the digitalization of the audiovisual media and Internet, offers opportunities for production, distribution, access and participation of the media products which must be urgently exploited.
- The present situation of the process of European integration, with the prospects of the expansion of the number of its members and the widening of the competencies of the Union, seems an especially opportune moment to bring together the measures which promote diversity, a real characteristic of the European culture, with the necessary strengthening of identity.

Of course globalization has many impacts on local culture worldwide. One of the positive aspects is that there is a spreading of information, there is cultural exchange and this can lead to a cultural growth worldwide. But there also is another aspect of cultural globalization: many see globalization of culture as an Americanization of different cultures. We can come up with *Disneyfication* (some authors call this phenomenon of "Disneyisation"), which is parallel to *McDonaldization,* mainly in the cultural and the artistic field of consumer society. According to this trend the world resembles a Disneyland-style theme park more and more. It is a nice, sweet, entertaining world without problems, a world without real life. Everything looks the same as if it was produced from a single assembly line. It is similar for today's mass culture.

Critics mention some aspects of Disneyfication: a) the concentration and growth of the power of Western popular culture (the relevance of the regional and smaller cultures is decreasing); b) everything is stereotyped, looks similar; c) exporting the Western perception of entertainment to the whole world and supporting consumerism under the slogan "buy, buy, buy!"; d) it has implications not only in culture but in architecture and society in general.

The other phenomenon in this category is commercialization which means the adaptation of media content to the wishes of the popular audience and to the wishes of advertisers. The volume of advertising in the context of globalisation is close to 350-400 billion dollars, the financial volume of the whole media business is much greater. Now, the advertising market is at the same time controlled by only a few "superad agency-owning companies." New media contents and formats are being produced and they are the face of this commercialization (reality shows, series and movie production). The primary principle is to produce a successful product aimed at a large audience.

Similarly, youth are the subject of a massive cultural assault from the unending flow of American television, magazines, books, films and music which bombard them daily. Here, culture is defined as 'a learned system of meaning and symbolizing which defines the unique identity of a people'.

The last process that changes the face of media and culture in these times at the turn of the millennium is the so-called cultural imperialism. In assessing this The Latest Globalisation Trends in Media phenomenon, we can start with the encyclopedia definition—it is the practice of promoting the culture and language of one nation or country in another country. The smaller culture is to be absorbed by the bigger, economically, militarily or politically stronger one. Since the 18th and 19th centuries we can highlight the promotion of the English language culture and the growing power of corporations as the most distinct manifestation of cultural imperialism. Even so, during the course of the 20th century other cases of cultural imperialism occurred as well. We can mention the Chinese repression of the Tibetan culture or the actions of the Soviet Union in the former Eastern bloc states. We should stress, however, that these processes were based on completely different premises and were executed in a violent way without the consent of these nations. Today the largest exponents of the "new form of cultural imperialism" are the countries of the West and the US. The principle of this phenomenon is the spread and the "gate-keeping" of information as well as the entertainment industry.

[…]

Conclusion

Considering the advantages and disadvantages of globalisation in the light of the analysis that has been done in the context of this paper, my argument is that much as globalisation may be inevitable, its consequences are devastating. It is therefore, my contention that, there is the need for an appropriate response in a view to understanding the dynamics that will hopefully help to evolve measures that will reduce the devastating effects of globalisation. In recent decades, media rhetoric has promoted the vision of a world in process of unification, largely as a result of technology's power to dissolve borders and speed communication. However, perspectives on globalization differ sharply, and these differences have been well defined by numerous analysts, some of whom have pointed to flaws in some of the more optimistic scenarios. A consideration of the role of media is highly important for the whole concept of globalization, but in theoretical debates these fields are largely ignored. The blindingly obvious point that there is no globalization without media has not been articulated or analysed clearly enough. The role of media is often reduced either to an exclusively and self-evidently technological one or to individuals' experiences that are unconnected to the media industries. Nevertheless, the two approaches are not mutually exclusive, because the production of media and the experience of them are linked, often in highly subtle ways.

Despite such dystopian warnings, it can be argued that the possibly dire effects of globalization are often concealed by glib rhetoric and powerful mythologies. Whatever facts may qualify it, the idea of a single interconnected world has become a necessary article of faith, an uplifting vision. Or, to put it another way, old dreams of a worldwide Utopia seem now to have meshed with opportunistic economic factors and to have been made fully realizable by the new technologies. However, mundane the reality of the trends, there is little theoretical interaction between globalization and media scholars. On the one hand, most globalization theorists come outside media and communication studies and have not studied media per se. On the other hand, most media scholars themselves have been occupied mainly with media economy and questions of power and inequality, as numerous books on international communication show. These issues are important but are not the only ones: globalization theorists have raised many issues which cannot be reduced solely to questions of economy and which most international communication scholars have ignored.

The world as a global village has come to stay. An institution that fails to meet the challenges of globalization shall remain irrelevant. There is no other lexis. This is the prize of globalization.

Exposure to Global Social Media Networks Can Change Traditional Local Cultures

Sean D. Young, Abbas Shakiba, Justin Kwok, and Mohammad Sadegh Montazeri

Sean D. Young and Justin Kwok are affiliated with the University of California, Los Angeles. Abbas Shakiba and Mohammad Sadegh Montazeri are affiliated with the University of Shahid Chamran and the University of Semnan, respectively, both in Iran.

Social networking technologies can influence attitudes, behaviors, and social norms. Research on this topic has been conducted primarily among early adopters of technology and within the United States. However, it is important to evaluate how social media might affect people's behaviors in international settings, especially among countries with longstanding, government recommended, cultural and religious traditions and behaviors, such as Iran. This study seeks to assess whether Iranian women who have been using social networking technologies for a longer time (compared to those who have recently joined) would be less likely to cover themselves with a veil and be more comfortable publicly displaying pictures of this behavior on Facebook. Iranian females ($N=253$) were selected through snowball sampling from nongovernmental organizations in November 2011 and asked to complete a survey assessing their use of Facebook, concerns about not wearing a veil in Facebook pictures, and their actual likelihood of wearing a veil. Items were combined to measure lack of interest in wearing a veil. Length of time as a Facebook user was significantly associated with not wearing a veil ($b=0.16$, $p<0.01$), controlling for age, education, and frequency of using

"The Influence of Social Networking Technologies on Female Religious Veil-Wearing Behavior in Iran", by Sean D. Young, Abbas Shakiba, Justin Kwok, and Mohammad Sadegh Montazeri, Mary Ann Liebert, Inc., May 1, 2014. Reprinted with permission from CYBERPSYCHOLOGY and BEHAVIOR, by Young et al, Published by Mary Ann Liebert, Inc., New Rochelle, NY

Facebook. Results also revealed a significant relationship such that older people were more likely to adhere to the religious behavior of wearing a veil ($b=-0.45$, $p<0.01$). Social networking technologies can affect attitudes and behaviors internationally. We discuss methods of using social media for self-presentation and expression, as well as the difficulties (and importance) of studying use of technologies, such as social media, internationally.

Introduction

Rapid growth in the use of online social networking has allowed these platforms to be used as technological tools for changing religious, political, and economic attitudes and behaviors.[1-3] With Facebook alone, recently reporting nearly 1.2 billion active monthly users and 728 million active daily users,[4] it becomes important to study and understand the implications of the global reach and influence of social networking technologies. Social networking platforms allow users to communicate globally and learn from people from various cultures, religious ideologies, and political affiliations. Social media have made a particular impact on providing access to information and communication among people living in countries with restricted media, such Iran.[5]

Online social networking technology usage has already been associated with social and behavioral norm formation and change in a variety of domains such as health,[6] politics,[7,8] and fashion.[9] Research on the relationship between social networking content and perceived social norms suggests that content on Facebook news feeds and friends' profiles impact people's attitudes and behaviors.[10] For example, researchers studying the effect of social media content on college drinking norms had participants view Facebook profiles that included or did not include alcohol-related content and asked them to report their perceptions of alcohol use. Those exposed to the alcohol experimental group estimated that the average student drank more frequently and in higher quantities than those in the control group.[11] Despite societal norms against binge drinking and risky sexual behaviors, social networking technologies had an effect on users' perceived social norms, leading them to engage in behaviors prevalent among their social network.[10,12]

Social networking technologies might also affect social and behavioral attitudes and norms in global settings. The majority of work on social networking technologies and behavioral norms has been conducted among early adopters of technology within the United States, a group and location that values change and adaptation.[13] However, research on this topic might be particularly interesting and important in countries with restrictive governments, such as Iran, where the ability to use social media might be rapidly changing the longstanding cultural and religious traditions. For instance, recent research suggests that social networking technologies provide citizens of Arab countries facing societal, cultural, and political limitations a platform for expressing their beliefs and values.[14] Results from one study suggested that individualism, adherence to traditions and values, and masculinity were significantly associated with the attitudes of Facebook members from those regions. The authors concluded that social networking sites have the ability to increase freedom of speech and reduce the effects of traditional cultural values that limit free social interaction.[14] Although numerous news, popular culture articles, and blogs suggest that social media affect the cultural and religious attitudes and behaviors of people living in Middle Eastern countries with restrictive governments,[5,15–17] this work has not been researched or published in academic journals.

Social media use within Middle Eastern countries has grown exponentially in recent years, and has been the driving force behind many societal changes in the Middle East, such as gender reform.[18] More notably, social networking sites played an integral role in the 2011 "Arab Spring" political protests, leading to the mobilization of many young adults.[19] Due to the growth of social media as a vehicle for change, many Middle Eastern governments began trying to preserve traditional and religious values.[20] However, despite the enormous social, political, and cultural implications of the increased use of social media, few studies have attempted (or have been able) to document the effects of social media on social norms and behavior in these regions.

In Iran, for example, social media use might be associated with women's interest in wearing a veil (hijab), a government-recommended cultural and religious tradition that has existed for more than 30 years.[21] In an attempt to display individualism, social networking users often avoid traditions such as religion[22] and cultural behaviors.[23] Similarly, female Iranians who have been using social networking sites for an extended period of time might prefer to avoid wearing a veil, as well as to avoid displaying themselves wearing a veil in their social media pictures. However, no research has studied this topic.

Methods

This study received a waiver of consent from the University of California, Los Angeles, institutional review board. An initial sample of 25 females at a university in Iran were approached and asked to complete a 15-item questionnaire on their use of Facebook, attitudes and beliefs about religious customs (including wearing a veil in pictures displayed on social media), and their likelihood of using drugs and engaging in sexual behaviors. Although initially approved by the local university in Iran, we were asked to remove the sex- and drug-related content in the questionnaire and to move to a different location.

The drug- and sex-related items were removed, and new sites were chosen. Female participants ($N=253$) were selected through snowball sampling from nongovernmental organizations (NGOs) in November 2011. Due to the nationwide ban on social networking Web sites, many social networking users have a strong desire to remain anonymous. Snowball sampling was determined to be the most effective way to sample participants in order to locate the hidden population of Facebook users. Three family cultural centers, as well as multiple public parks in Isfahan City, Iran, were chosen initially. Participants were approached at these locations, given a leaflet, and asked if they would like to participate in the study. Leaflets contained the following: (a) information about the goal of the study; (b) a statement ensuring that participants and their answers would remain fully anonymous; and (c) a link to the online survey. All surveys were completely anonymous, and results were saved to a secure database. Participants were then asked to pass the leaflet to friends and acquaintances who might be interested in participating in the survey. Participants were not paid for their involvement in the study.

Measures

Due to participants' desire to remain anonymous and not be contacted again, it was not possible to conduct a randomized controlled trial or to sample participants at multiple time points. Therefore, one cross-sectional survey was conducted where we attempted to measure the influence of having a Facebook account over time by measuring associations with the age of participants' Facebook accounts. The basic demographic information we asked of our participants included their age and level of education. Participants were also asked to report the amount of time they had had a Facebook account, the amount of time they used the Internet on a daily basis, and the number of friends they had on Facebook. All data gathered from participants were through self-report. The amount of time as a Facebook user was measured in months, and daily time spent on the Internet was measured in hours.

Participants were also asked a number of questions about their religious veil-related attitudes and behaviors. Wearing the veil incorrectly according to religious tradition is known as "keeping improper hijab." To attempt to measure change over time, we asked participants how those attitudes and behaviors might have changed compared to 6 months ago. For example, participants were asked, "In comparison to 6 months ago, how likely are you to post Facebook pictures showing that you do not properly wear your veil?" (5-point Likert scale where 1="very unlikely" and 5="very likely"), and "In comparison to 6 months ago, how worried are you that others see and criticize your level of wearing a veil in Facebook in pictures?" (5-point Likert scale where 1="not at all worried" and 5="very worried"). We also asked participants how likely it was that they would feel embarrassed knowing that their photos are seen either by friends or strangers (5-point Likert scale where 1="not at all worried" and 5="very worried"). Lastly, we asked participants, "In comparison to the last 6 months, how likely are you to put more photos with improper hijab on your Facebook profile?" (5-point Likert scale where 1="not at all worried" and 5="very worried"). Cronbach's alpha reliability coefficient was calculated to assess the internal consistency of the seven questions assessing adherence to the traditional Islamic custom. Items had a high internal consistency rating (Cronbach's $\alpha=0.90$). The seven items were summed together and combined to measure general lack of observing traditional veil covering in pictures displayed on Facebook.

Results

Participants were on average almost 22 years old, with more than 30% being educated to high school level or below. More than 40% of women earned a bachelor's degree or higher level of education. Activities that participants carried out the most on Facebook were checking updates of their Facebook friends (17.4%) and using Facebook groups (19.4%). The average participant joined Facebook about 1 year prior to the survey, and used Facebook for more than 3 hours a day.

Compared to 6 months earlier, participants were on average slightly less likely to be embarrassed if Facebook friends saw pictures of them wearing an improper hijab ($M=3.39$, $SD=0.97$). Compared to 6 months earlier, participants felt slightly less embarrassed knowing that strangers on Facebook would see photos of them without a proper hijab ($M=3.45$, $SD=0.96$). The respondents were also slightly less worried that others would criticize their levels of observing traditional Islamic customs of the hijab ($M=3.60$, $SD=0.87$). Women on average reported they would be slightly more likely to upload photos with an improper hijab in the future (*M*=3.26, *SD*=0.88). Participants also stated that, compared to the past 6 months, they felt less prohibited in uploading photos with an improper hijab onto Facebook (*M*=3.36, *SD*=0.97).

There was a significant positive correlation between keeping improper hijab and time having a Facebook account (*b*=0.16, *p*=0.005), controlling for age, education, and daily amount of time using Facebook. Results also revealed a significant negative correlation between the participant's age (*b*=−0.240, *p*<0.01) and keeping improper hijab, as well as a significant positive relationship between keeping improper hijab and daily amount of time using Facebook (*b*=0.23, *p*<0.01). No significant relationship was found between level of educational attainment and likelihood of observing religious traditions.

Discussion

Results suggest that use of Facebook can affect Iranian women's perceptions about and likelihood of engaging in a traditional Iranian religious behavior—the wearing of a head veil. These findings support research suggesting that social media users value personal identity, individualism, and avoiding traditional factors such as religion and culture.[22,23] As time spent on Facebook increases, it is likely that exposure to different cultures and beliefs increases, shaping people's perceptions of social norms. This work also builds on research suggesting that social media affects attitudes and behaviors[9,10] by investigating how Facebook might affect Iranian women's attitudes and behaviors about engaging in longstanding cultural and religious traditions.

As social networking technologies continue to grow, and as researchers continue to find more ways to study countries with restrictive access, it will be interesting to investigate more thoroughly how social media and other technologies impact people's attitudes and behaviors. In the United States, for example, people of almost all age groups, religious ideologies, and political affiliations use social networking sites, exposing users to multiple ideologies and beliefs in addition to the norms prevalent in their own networks. In Iran, populations currently using social networking sites are primarily younger individuals with higher education levels and similar political views, which is representative of only a segment of the population. Those actively involved on social networking sites are possibly exposed to foreign ideas and values, influencing their attitudes and behaviors. However, in the future, it is conceivable that as Iranians with more conservative views begin using social networking technologies, the experience will become more like that of the United States where users are exposed to all types of social norms and not just specific to the groups one joins.

Although this study finds that longer term use of social networking technologies is associated with reduced likelihood of wearing a veil in Facebook pictures among Iranian women, it is possible that results may be different in other Middle Eastern countries. For example, in the historically secular Middle Eastern country of Turkey, women have been increasingly wearing a veil by choice, and the veil has become a sign of following popular trends.[24] In Turkey, use of social networking technologies might therefore be associated with increased observance of wearing a veil. Future research can explore these issues to determine how social norms may differ among countries with strong cultural and/ or religious traditions and how social networking technology use affects attitudes and behaviors among people in those countries.

There are several limitations of this research, most of which are a result of government restrictions and our respect to observe these rules and participant needs. For example, due to participant concerns regarding being contacted again, we were unable to conduct a randomized controlled trial or measure multiple time points to determine change in wearing a veil over time as a result of Facebook use. However, this study provides an initial methodology that can be used to research attitudes and behaviors in Iran and other countries with similar politics. Additionally, we believe the present study is an initial approach at demonstrating an unstudied and interesting effect on how social media can affect attitudes internationally. Future research might explore this question using more controlled methods by studying this question in other countries. We found it was much more difficult to conduct this research than it has been for us to conduct research in other international settings, including difficultly in accessing participants, conforming to and respecting government recommendations, and ensuring the comfort and safety of research participants. However, we believe this study is important in providing a call for researchers to begin studying the effects of social media internationally while being able to respect the wishes of different types of governments. As social media and access to information and people continue to grow in countries such as Iran, it will become easier for researchers to study the impact of technologies on citizens of those countries and help us to understand whether and how technologies can be used to improve the lives of people in these countries.

This study provides initial support that, among Iranian woman, social media use is associated with reduced concerns about adhering to veil-related social norms and behaviors on social media. Because of the lack of research on this topic and within these regions, this study aims to provide a call for future research to understand better how technology might impact cultural and religious changes in important international settings.

References

1. Hanson G, Haridakis PM, Cunningham AW, et al. The 2008 presidential campaign: political cynicism in the age of Facebook, MySpace, and YouTube. Mass Communication & Society 2010; 13:584–607

2. Obar JA, Zube P, Lampe C. Advocacy 2.0: an analysis of how advocacy groups in the United States perceive and use social media as tools for facilitating civic engagement and collective action. Journal of Information Policy 2012; 2:1–25

3. Newnham J, Bell P. Social network media and political activism: a growing challenge for law enforcement. Journal of Policing, Intelligence & Counter Terrorism 2012; 7:36–50

4. Facebook (2013) Facebook reports third quarter 2013 results [Press Release]. http://investor.fb.com/releasedetail.cfm?ReleaseID=802760 (accessed Nov. 25, 2013)

5. Sohrabi-Haghighat MH. New media and social-political change in Iran. Online Journal of the Virtual Middle East 2011; 5 www.cyberorient.net/article. do?articleId=6187 (accessed Nov. 21, 2013)

6. Neiger BL, Thackeray R, Burton SH, et al. Evaluating social media's capacity to develop engaged audiences in health promotion settings: use of Twitter metrics as a case study. Health Promotion Practice2013; 14:157–162 [PubMed]

7. Vitak J, Zube P, Smock A, et al. It's complicated: Facebook users' political participation in the 2008 election. CyberPsychology, Behavior, & Social Networking 2011; 14:107–114 [PubMed]

8. Zhang W, Johnson TJ, Seltzer T, et al. The revolution will be networked: the influence of social networking sites on political attitudes and behavior. Social Science Computer Review 2010; 28:75–92

9. Phan M, Thomas R, Heine K. Social media and luxury brand management: the case of Burberry. Journal of Global Fashion Marketing 2011; 2:213–222

10. Young SD, Jordan AH. The influence of social networking photos on social norms and sexual health behaviors. CyberPsychology, Behavior, & Social Networking 2013; 16:243–247 [PMC free article][PubMed]

11. Fournier AK, Hall E, Ricke P, et al. Alcohol and the social network: online social networking sites and college students' perceived drinking norms. Psychology of Popular Media Culture 2013; 2:86–95

12. Wechsler H, Nelson TF, Lee JE, et al. Perception and reality: a national evaluation of social norms marketing interventions to reduce college students' heavy alcohol use. Journal of Studies on Alcohol and Drugs 2003; 64:484–494 [PubMed]

13. Centola D. The spread of behavior in an online social network experiment. Science 2010; 329:1194–1197 [PubMed]

14. Omoush A, Saleh K, Yaseen SG, et al. The impact of Arab cultural values on online social networking: the case of Facebook. Computers in Human Behavior 2012; 28:2387–2399

15. Chatfield AT, Akbari R, Mirzayi N, et al. (2012) Interactive effects of networked publics and social media on transforming the public sphere: a survey of Iran's leaderless "social media revolution." In System Science (HICSS) 2012; 45th Hawaii International Conference on System Sciences, Kauai, Hawaii

16. Salem F, Mourtada R. (2012) Social media in the Arab world: influencing societal and cultural change? Arab Social Media Report. www.arabsocialmediareport. com/UserManagement/PDF/ASMR%204%20updated%2029%2008%2012.pdf (accessed Nov. 21, 2013)

17. Bunt GR. Virtually Islamic. http://virtuallyislamic.blogspot.com/2013_09_01_archive.html (accessed Nov. 21, 2013)

18. Al-Ali N. (2000) Secularism, gender and the state in the Middle East: the Egyptian women's movement. Cambridge, United Kingdom: Cambridge University Press

19. Rahimi B. (2007). The politics of the Internet in Iran. Media, culture and society in Iran: living with globalization and the Islamic state. New York: Routledge

20. Freedom House (2011) Freedom of the Net (p. 410). www.freedomhouse.org/sites/default/files/FOTN2011.pdf (accessed Nov. 21, 2013)

21. Hoodfar H. (1999) The women's movement in Iran: women at the crossroads of secularization and Islamization. In: Women living under Muslim laws (Organization). France: Grabels Cedex, p. 49

22. Hjarvard S. The mediatisation of religion: Theorising religion, media and social change. Culture & Religion 2011; 12:119–135

23. De Angeli A. Cultural variations in virtual spaces design. AI & Society 2009; 24:213–223

24. Gökarıksel B, Secor AJ. New transnational geographies of Islamism, capitalism and subjectivity: the veiling fashion industry in Turkey. Area 2009; 41:6–18

Chapter 4

Does Economic Globalization Contribute to Poverty?

Globalization's Rise Has Been Accompanied by Changes in Inequality and Poverty

Baylee Molloy

Baylee Molloy served as a research and writing fellow at the Institute for Faith, Work, and Economics. She is a graduate of the University of Virginia with a master's degree in public policy.

Does globalization negatively or positively impact poverty alleviation?

According to economist Pranab Bardhan,

> Antiglobalizers' central claim is that globalization is making the rich richer and the poor poorer; [while] proglobalizers assert that it actually helps the poor.

By definition, globalization is the increasing integration of world economies through the expansion of trade, investment, technology, labor, and knowledge.

The impact of globalization on the poor is not a black or white issue. Making a direct causal impact between globalization and poverty reduction is difficult.

According to economic and political writer Doug Bandow,

> Some critics of globalization have contended that the process has helped the rich and hurt the poor. However, the best research indicates that this is not accurate: 'Poverty is falling rapidly in those poor countries that are integrating into the global economy.'

In order to understand how globalization *can* positively affect the poor, we must understand recent changes to poverty and inequality. We must also understand how individual countries' domestic policies impact globalization's effects.

"Does Globalization Harm the Poor?" by Baylee Molloy, Institute for Faith, Work & Economics, April 4, 2016. Reprinted by permission. This article is reprinted with permission from the Institute for Faith, Work & Economics (www.tifwe.org). The original article appears at https://tifwe.org/does-globalization-harm-the-poor/. IFWE is a Christian research organization committed to advancing biblical and economic principles that help individuals find fulfillment in their work and contribute to a free and flourishing society. Visit https://tifwe.org/subscribe to subscribe to the free IFWE Daily Blog.

Global Poverty Reduced

Poverty rates around the world are decreasing as more countries continue integrating into the global economy.

In 2011 *Yale Global* reported:

Today, we estimate that there are approximately 820 million people living on less than $1.25 a day. This means that the prime target of the Millennium Development Goals... was probably achieved around three years ago.

Globalization opens markets, spreads the use of new technology, and expands division of labor.

Division of labor helps societies grow economically. When countries become a part of a more globalized economy, they are able to more finely tune their comparative advantage. This leads to greater productivity and unlocks flourishing in the long run as countries are able to trade goods and services with one another freely.

Large numbers of people have been raised out of extreme poverty over the past few decades, particularly in India, China, and Indonesia. Bardhan states,

Between 1981 and 2001 the percentage of rural people living on less than $1 a day decreased from 79 to 27 percent in China, 63 to 42 percent in India, and 55 to 11 percent in Indonesia.

Globalization has helped these countries develop by integrating their economies with the rest of the world. The openness of these countries has provided their poor with greater access to capital, knowledge, and opportunities.

While Bandow acknowledges that economists find it difficult to prove causation between international openness and economic growth, he quotes economists Jeffrey Sachs and Andrew Warner's research stating:

We find strong association between openness and growth... within the group of developing countries, the open economies grew at 4.49 percent per year, and the closed economies grew at 0.69 percent per year.

Industries and jobs may be displaced in the short run as a result of globalization and trade as economies begin to experience growth, but, in the long run, both employment opportunities and consumption will increase.

Economist David Henderson's recent research shows that globalization benefits the poor by lowering the costs of goods they typically consume.

Countries taking part in the global economy are experiencing more economic growth and poverty reduction than those countries which remain in isolation.

What About Inequality?

What about inequality? Critics of globalization argue that it increases inequality in poorer countries.

In *The Economist*, an article arguing that globalization does not reduce inequality uses the Gini index to measure inequality.

> [The Gini index is] based on a score between zero and one. A Gini index of one means a country's entire income goes to one person; a score of zero means the spoils are equally divided. Sub-Saharan Africa saw its Gini index rise by 9% between 1993 and 2008. China's score soared by 34% over twenty years. Only in a few places has it fallen.

This means that inequality in developing countries has generally risen over the past two to three decades.

While it has been challenging for economists to make a direct correlation between globalization and poverty reduction or increases/decreases in inequality, the *Economist* article provides one theory for how globalization creates high inequality:

> Outsourcing—when rich countries shift parts of the production process to poor countries. Contrary to popular belief, multinationals in poor countries often employ skilled workers and pay high wages. One study showed that workers in foreign-owned and subcontracting clothing and footwear factories in Vietnam rank in the top 20% of the country's population by household expenditure. A report from the OECD found that

average wages paid by foreign multinationals are 40% higher than wages paid by local firms… By contrast, unskilled workers, or poor ones in rural areas, tend not to have such opportunities… For these reasons globalization can boost the wages of skilled workers, while crimping those of the unskilled. The result is that inequality rises.

From this point of view, we can see how globalization may be a contributor to inequality. However, there are two things that we should keep in mind: (1) the impact tends to be relatively small, and (2) income inequality is not necessarily a negative thing.

Studying the impact of technology, trade, and financial globalization on income inequality, the IMF found that:

The contribution of increased globalization to inequality has in general been relatively minor. This reflects two offsetting effects of globalization: while increased trade tends to reduce income inequality, foreign direct investment tends to exacerbate it.

Bandow tells us that according to the World Bank, changes in inequality are usually small and globalization contributes to positive changes in the developing world:

Most of the globalizing developing countries have seen only small changes in household inequality, and inequality has declined in such countries as the Philippines and Malaysia. Moreover, greater economic openness to the world has tended to reduce gender inequality.

Anne Bradley argues that income inequality can actually be a sign of a robust economy. It's not, of course, when inequality forms as a result of exploitation, but when it comes from trade that means greater specialization from markets and more trading partners. In an article on poverty and inequality, Bradley states,

Income inequality deals with how income is held over a society. Unless everyone is exactly equal, there will always be a top and a bottom. What matters is how the folks at the bottom fare and whether they have opportunities to use their God-given creativity and skills to give them income mobility.

Globalization can allow just that: an expansion of opportunities for those at the bottom which provides greater economic and social mobility.

Additionally, where inequalities do arise, the gap is typically not the result of globalization, but rather domestic government policies that dampen the positive impacts globalization could have brought.

Why Domestic Policies Matter

A concern for those looking at the impact of globalization is that while countries in Asia seem to be doing well in terms of poverty reductions, countries in places such as sub-Saharan Africa are not performing as well. Bardhan presents us with the following data:

> Between 1981 and 2001 the fraction of Africans living below the international poverty line increased from 42 to 47 percent.

This result has less to do with globalization's negative impacts and more to do with the country's political regime and domestic policies.

Ann Harrison, a research associate with the National Bureau of Economic Research, states,

> The poor will indeed benefit from globalization if the appropriate complementary policies and institutions are in place.

Bardhan points out that,

> Opening markets without relieving these domestic constraints forces people to compete with one hand tied behind their back. The result can be deepened poverty.

Countries where regimes are unstable, the poor lack rule of law (land rights, justice in the court, freedom to start a business), and corruption is widespread create major limitations for the poor across the world.

In order for globalization to work, countries need to introduce domestic reforms and actually implement them. Reforms in areas such as rule of law would benefit countries seeking to gain from globalization and would help reduce poverty.

Bandow states,

> Without sound domestic policies, it will be difficult to attract foreign investment and generate long-term economic growth… Still, greater foreign openness is likely to encourage greater domestic reform.

Often times those that say globalization negatively impacts the poor believe that the best way to improve the impact of globalization is through greater global regulatory arrangements. However, Bardhan would argue that opening up a country to globalization itself is what will help a country improve. He states,

> If we keep the focus on agitating against transnational companies and international organizations like the WTO, attention in those countries often gets deflected from the domestic institutional vested interests, and the day of politically challenging them gets postponed… [Instead] opening the economy may unleash forces for such a challenge… [global competition] may be a force bringing about improvements in accountability of hitherto elite-dominated governance institutions.

Countries opening up to trade will be influenced by trade, technology, and ideas. These factors challenge the status quo and can lead to significant reform.

While income inequalities may arise from increased global competition, income mobility will be positively affected by globalization providing the poor with more opportunity. Additionally, the long-term effects of globalization provide the poor with better standards of living as they gain more access to improved market goods.

When a country opens itself up to the world market, globalization can become a positive mechanism for increasing economic opportunity and unleashing flourishing for the least of these.

Free Trade Does Not Increase Wealth and Prosperity Equally

Anthony Amoah

Anthony Amoah is an applied economist and senior lecturer at the Central University, Ghana. He is a member of the Royal Economic Society in the UK.

International trade is essential to every economy of the world today as a result of factor endowment supply differences. However, policy-wise there has been an intense debate on the extent for which trade should be free. This debate has taken the center stage of analysis for international economists. This essay provides evidence to justify the debate for and against free trade in the context of helping the educated, and exploiting poor workers in developing countries. This essay provides evidence that free trade has helped the educated in developing countries however, it has also hurt and exploited the poor worker. We recommend a certain level of restriction to control for the extent of exploitation.

Introduction

Trade practice is an old economic concept that has existed with humankind and still is. This phenomenon of transactions and exchange is described by Todaro and Smith (2009) as a basic component of human activity throughout the world. This is principally explained by the resource or factor endowment supply differences. With time, trade has seen a holistic evolution in its composition, direction and policies or laws. Numerous studies have sought to establish a relationship between trade and other policy areas including labour relations, human rights, and competition policy. However, these hardly include a precise definition of free

"Does Free Trade Predominantly Lead to the Exploitation of Workers and Benefit Only the Economic Elite in Developing Countries?" by Anthony Amoah, Norwich Economic Papers, June 2015. Reprinted by permission.

trade (Driesen, 2000). Scholars are believed to have assumed that free trade definition is obvious by its name. Phrases such as trade barriers (see Bhagwati, 1996), trade restrictions (see Farber and Hudec, 1996), and protectionism (see Nanda, 1995; Sykes, 1999; Bhagwati, 2002) are used in the literature to describe that which trade should be free of (Driesen, 2000). There is therefore a dearth of evidence regarding the precise definition of free trade across disciplines as the word 'free' is quite subjective.

Generally, international economists in a more simplistic way describe free trade as an economic policy that does not restrict buying and selling of goods and services between countries without the imposition of constraints such as tariffs, duties and quotas. In another broader sense, Henderson (1992) defines free trade as freedom to engage in international transactions without discriminations (see Sally, 2008). These definitions conform to the laissez-faire definition of free trade which has it that there should be absolute license (i.e. trade without burdens or restrictions). According to Charnovitz (1994, p.463) "the current status of what is widely known as free trade, i.e. the 'free' and unregulated movement of goods and services around the globe, is an unacceptable status quo." Many scholars and commentators have expressed the idea that free trade description should have a moral baseline. Cooper (1994) argues that "the international community cannot, and should not be able to, force a country to purchase products the production of which offends the sensibilities of its citizenry." Drucker (1997) sees the need for "moral, legal, and economic rules that are accepted and enforced throughout the global economy." Also, Henry George, a leading free trader of the 19th century, argued in favour of moral exception when he explained that, "Free trade, its true meaning, requires not merely the abolition of protection but the sweeping away of all tariffs—the abolition of all restrictions (save those imposed in the interests of public health or morals) on the bring" (Charnovitz, 1997, p.689).

Irrespective of the description of free trade, it is important to note that since the era of barter system, the idea of trading has come to stay by its overwhelming acceptance by individual nations and the international community, albeit, few countries have anything approaching completely free trade (Krugman et al., 2012). This is explained mainly by its merits and demerits which has resulted in debates amongst international economists, policy makers and governments. The free trade debate which has taken the center stage of analysis for international economists dates back to the concept of division of labour as discussed by Adam Smith and David Ricardo, following James Mill, developed the theory of comparative advantage and justified the theoretical essence of free trade (Bhagwati, 1994).

Despite the direction of this debate and whichever definition is generally acceptable, the role of the international community in free trade cannot be overemphasized. After the Second World War, there has been international coordination in promoting Globalization and free trade policies which saw the establishment of several international institutions such as the World Bank, International Monetary Fund (IMF), General Agreement on Tariffs and Trade (GATT). In 1995, the worldwide GATT agreement also set up a new organisation which, the World Trade Organisation (WTO) with the role of monitoring and promoting free trade in place of protectionism (Krugman et al., 2012).

In the context of this study, we define developing countries as those with low income, lower-middle income, and upper-middle income. This follows the World Bank classification of countries with per capita Gross National incomes in 2005 of $875 or less (low income or LIC); between $876 and $3465 (lower-middle income or MIC); between $3466 and $10725 (upper-middle income or MIC) and $10726 or more (high income or HIC) (Todaro and Smith, 2009). For most developing countries, major trade reforms and liberalization policies seem not to have eroded the abject poverty they experience with its associated impact on labour or workers. The relationship between free trade, poverty and labour is crucial as it provides evidence on whether trade is beneficial for developing countries or otherwise. In a narrower sense, knowing the effect of free trade on labour in developing countries will provide evidence to determine if free trade has adverse effects on poor workers or benefit economic elites. It is from this point that investigations into a gap such as this are encouraged. Thus, this essay seeks to answer the following question: Does free trade exploit poor workers in developing countries or free trade helps the educated in developing countries?

Free Trade: Theoretical Justification

The theory underpinning free trade and its merits follows the seminal work "The Wealth of Nations" by Adam Smith. Subsequently, the free-trade model was developed by David Ricardo (building on John Stuart Mill) which was based on the principle that with specialization and division of labour, mutual gains are derived among trading nations (Bhagwati, 2002). This was a static model based on a one-variable-factor assumption (with constant productivity of labour in two goods, but with relative productivity between the goods different across countries) illustrating gains from trade through specialization (Todaro and Smith, 2009). By the 20th century Ricardian neoclassical theory was modified by Eli Hecksher and Bertil Ohlin (Hecksher- Ohlin). The Hecksher-Ohlin neoclassical theory took into account differences in factor[1] supplies on international trade hence the name Hecksher-Ohlin neoclassical factor endowment theory. This theory provides the basis for analysing the impact of economic growth on trade patterns and the impact of trade on the structure of national economies and on the differential returns or payments to various factors of production. They argue that the basis for trade principally centers on the different factor supplies of countries. Therefore countries with cheap labour are likely to have a relative cost and price advantage over countries with relatively expensive labour in commodities that make intensive use of labour.[2] Such countries are admonished to labour-intensive products and export surplus in return for products of capital-intensive goods. Also, countries endowed with capital are likely to have a relative cost and price advantage in commodities that make intensive use of capital.[3] They also tend to benefit from specialisation in and export of capital-intensive products.

Following the Ricardian and Heckscher-Ohlin theoretical propositions discussed, we sum the Ricardian comparative advantage as based on relative technological differences and Heckscher–Ohlin comparative advantage based on international differences in relative factor endowments. Thus, countries can benefit from free trade, even if they are less productive in every industry than other nations, or produce all goods more cheaply than other countries, each one would benefit by specializing in the export of its relatively cheapest good (Dutt, 2005; Miles & Scott, 2005). The argument of mutual benefits by countries being developed or developing provide support for the proposition by Bhagwati (2002) that "free trade is [an economic] policy that makes eminent sense."

Some Stylized Facts on Trade

The World Bank in 1996[4] acknowledged the possible impact trade between developing and the developed countries could make on the global economy. In 2009, the materialisation of this expectation was observed by Joseph Stiglitz. He indicated that developing countries have been part of the world's engine of economic growth, and it is hard to imagine a robust global recovery in which the developing countries did not play a role.

Overall, merchandise trade[5] in early sixties were not that much encouraging. In 1963 it rose from 22% to about 33% in 1980 and about 18% to 34% for low income and middle income countries respectively. In the same period, merchandise trade of high income countries (OECD only) rose from 16% to 32%. The free trade facilitation role by WTO (former GATT) in 1995 was strongly felt as overall merchandise trade recorded unprecedented average of about 36% of GDP. Thus, global trade grew rapidly in the 90s. Developing countries (low-income and middle-income countries) merchandised trade grew from (an average of about) 32% in 1993 to 53% in 2008. Developed countries represented here by high-income (OECD) countries increased from (about) 26% to 46% in 2008. These increases are attributed to the fact that significant increases in trade openness occurred in all regions (World Bank, 2012).The impact of the 2008 financial crises or better still recession was felt globally hence overall merchandise trade fell to an average of 41% of GDP in 2009.

The World Bank (2012, p.255) continues to argue that,

"Changes in foreign direct investment (FDI) have also been significant, with flows increasing from 0.5 percent of GDP in 1980 to 4 percent in 2007, followed by a decline during the recent financial crisis. As goods, services, capital, and people flow across countries faster than ever before, information and knowledge have become global commodities. Technological change crosses borders embedded in traded goods, accelerating its adoption and adaptation. And although technology transfers tend to happen first in exports and imports, they quickly spread beyond them as firms interact and workers change jobs. Similarly, ideas and skills move from one country to another as the share of skilled migrants in the pool of international migrants increases—from about 25 percent in 1990 to 36 percent in 2000"

In focus, it is important to re-emphasize that free trade is regarded as the key factor underlying this rise in trade evidenced by a positive trend in trade and a high GDP growth in developing countries.

Free Trade: Benefits to the Economic Elite and How It Hurts Poor Workers

This section is sub-divided into two sections namely: the benefits to economic elites, and how it hurts poor workers in developing countries. These are discussed below.

Free Trade Benefits Economic Elite in
Developing Countries: Justification

This section provides the economic benefits of free trade to economic elite in developing countries following the intuition of John Stuart Mill as outlined in his book on the *Principles of Political Economy* (1848).

First, the direct economic gains of free trade to economic elite. This basically explains the gains associated with specialisation as postulated by Smith and Ricardo. The degree to which economic elites specialize in certain tasks, enhances productivity. With productivity being the ability to produce more goods with the same resources, is the basis for higher wages and rising living standards. Considering the scarce nature of economic elite in developing countries, the ability to hire and use such scarce resources is associated with higher remuneration. Thus, domestic price for hiring labour to engage in the production of products with comparative advantage rises. In another breadth, the educated skilled labour is able to freely move to countries where their skills are very much needed. Here, the assumption is that marginal labour productivity is very much drawn upon, and its associated reward of higher wages and salaries is inevitable. In sum, higher wage rates and better living standards are expected to be characterised with economic elite in developing countries due to their scarce and free movement nature.

Secondly, indirect economic gains of free trade to economic elite. This concept suggests the tendency of every extension of the market to improve the processes of production. A developing country that produces for a larger market than its own can easily harness the benefits of division of labour. Free trade contributes to a process by which a firm can easily access and adopt a new technology needed to support the educated elite to be highly efficient. The skilled educated elite are able to complement perfectly on their specialised machines. This is more likely to promote efficiency through inventions/innovations and improvements in the production process. Once demand for such labour's services by firms is high, it's associated higher wages or salaries cannot be overemphasised. Thus, free trade appears to raise income [of the educated elite] through higher productivity which is achieved by spurring the accumulation of physical and human capital (Frankel & Romer, 1999).

Free Trade Exploits Poor Workers in Developing Countries: Justification

The extent to which free trade has been criticised dates back to the last two centuries following views expressed by John Maynard Keynes and John Hicks (Bhagwati, 2002).

To begin with, it is therefore generally recommended that for developing countries to engage in free trade, it would be ideal for them to maintain macroeconomic stability (Bhagwati and Srinivasan, 2002). However, achieving macroeconomic stability has been a big challenge for most developing countries. Developing countries are mostly characterised by high inflation rates and excess supply of unskilled labour. In the wake of free trade with free movement of factors of production especially unskilled labour, it will force market conditions to allocate lower wages for the services of the excess unskilled labour. Coupled with weak law enforcing institutions, firms will end up paying unskilled labour below the minimum wage hence worsening the plight of the poor worker.

The structure of educational systems in developing countries are not diverse and broad relative to developed countries. A lot more people end up being trained for similar if not same jobs with less opportunities. The free movement of factors of production especially labour is likely to increase the supply of skilled labour at the expense of unskilled labour. This will expose the unskilled to foreign competition in previously sheltered sectors. In such cases, jobs meant for unskilled labour will now be competed for even by skilled labour as a stop-gap measure in waiting to take jobs that fully require their skills.

Also, technical progress is argued to be biased against unskilled workers in developing countries and hence this bias in new technology widens wage differentials (Wood, 1995). Thus, it can be argued that if factor prices were fixed under a dominating labour-intensive economy just as in developing countries, the gap between skilled and unskilled wages would be widened by technical progress that was slower in labour-intensive than in skill-based-intensive sectors. This argument is justified because labour-intensive sectors would need to offset their growing technical disadvantage by restraining the wages of the majority of their workers.

Conclusion and Recommendation

This essay explains how free trade acts as a 'two edged sword'. This is achieved by explaining how in one breadth it affects economic elite positively and in another breadth it hurts poor workers in developing countries.

The theoretical and empirical evidence (see Frankel & Romer, 1999) of the potential of free trade increasing material prosperity among nations especially developing countries cannot be overlooked. However, as Boudreaux (2010) puts it, "While this argument is powerful and backed by overwhelming empirical support, it tends to leave many people cold. A common reaction to free-trade arguments might be: 'You economists care only about low prices and more stuff; there's more to life than *things*.'"

This essay therefore strongly supports the view that free trade is beneficial to developing countries. However, it is also quick to indicate that it is not without its excesses. We recommend better macroeconomic environment under free trade policies and better restriction to control for the extent of exploitation.

Notes

1 These are mainly Labour, Land and Capital

2 For example countries that engage in the production of primary products

3 For example countries that engage in the production of manufacturing goods

4 Read more: http://www.ukessays.co.uk/essays/economics/the-globalization-of-the-world-economy-economics-essay.php

5 As a percentage of Gross Domestic Product (% GDP)

Globalization Is a Factor in Increasing Inequality

Nikil Savil

Nikil Saval is an American writer, editor, and journalist. He is co-editor of n+1, *a magazine on literature, culture, and politics.*

The annual January gathering of the World Economic Forum in Davos is usually a placid affair: a place for well-heeled participants to exchange notes on global business opportunities, or powder conditions on the local ski slopes, while cradling champagne and canapes. This January, the ultra-rich and the sparkling wine returned, but by all reports the mood was one of anxiety, defensiveness and self-reproach.

The future of economic globalisation, for which the Davos men and women see themselves as caretakers, had been shaken by a series of political earthquakes. "Globalisation" can mean many things, but what lay in particular doubt was the long-advanced project of increasing free trade in goods across borders. The previous summer, Britain had voted to leave the largest trading bloc in the world. In November, the unexpected victory of Donald Trump, who vowed to withdraw from major trade deals, appeared to jeopardise the trading relationships of the world's richest country. Forthcoming elections in France and Germany suddenly seemed to bear the possibility of anti-globalisation parties garnering better results than ever before. The barbarians weren't at the gates to the ski-lifts yet—but they weren't very far.

In a panel titled Governing Globalisation, the economist Dambisa Moyo, otherwise a well-known supporter of free trade, forthrightly asked the audience to accept that "there have been significant losses" from globalisation. "It is not clear to me that we are going to be able to remedy them under the current

"Globalisation: The Rise and Fall of An Idea That Swept the World," by Nikil Saval, Guardian News and Media Limited, July 14, 2017. Reprinted by permission.

infrastructure," she added. Christine Lagarde, the head of the International Monetary Fund, called for a policy hitherto foreign to the World Economic Forum: "more redistribution." After years of hedging or discounting the malign effects of free trade, it was time to face facts: globalisation caused job losses and depressed wages, and the usual Davos proposals—such as instructing affected populations to accept the new reality—weren't going to work. Unless something changed, the political consequences were likely to get worse.

The backlash to globalisation has helped fuel the extraordinary political shifts of the past 18 months. During the close race to become the Democratic party candidate, senator Bernie Sanders relentlessly attacked Hillary Clinton on her support for free trade. On the campaign trail, Donald Trump openly proposed tilting the terms of trade in favour of American industry. "Americanism, not globalism, shall be our creed," he bellowed at the Republican national convention last July. The vote for Brexit was strongest in the regions of the UK devastated by the flight of manufacturing. At Davos in January, British prime minister Theresa May, the leader of the party of capital and inherited wealth, improbably picked up the theme, warning that, for many, "talk of greater globalisation … means their jobs being outsourced and wages undercut." Meanwhile, the European far right has been warning against free movement of people as well as goods. Following her qualifying victory in the first round of France's presidential election, Marine Le Pen warned darkly that "the main thing at stake in this election is the rampant globalisation that is endangering our civilisation."

It was only a few decades ago that globalisation was held by many, even by some critics, to be an inevitable, unstoppable force. "Rejecting globalisation," the American journalist George Packer has written, "was like rejecting the sunrise." Globalisation could take place in services, capital and ideas, making it a notoriously imprecise term; but what it meant most often was making it cheaper to trade across borders—something that seemed to many at the time to be an unquestionable good. In practice, this often meant that industry would move from rich countries, where labour was expensive, to poor countries, where labour was cheaper. People in the rich countries would either have to accept lower wages to compete, or lose their jobs. But no matter what, the goods they formerly produced would now be imported, and be even cheaper. And the unemployed could get new, higher-skilled jobs (if they got the requisite training). Mainstream economists and politicians upheld the consensus about the merits of globalisation, with little concern that there might be political consequences.

Back then, economists could calmly chalk up anti-globalisation sentiment to a marginal group of delusional protesters, or disgruntled stragglers still toiling uselessly in "sunset industries". These days, as sizable constituencies have voted in country after country for anti-free-trade policies, or candidates that promise to limit them, the old self-assurance is gone. Millions have rejected, with uncertain results, the punishing logic that globalisation could not be stopped. The backlash has swelled a wave of soul-searching among economists, one that had already begun to roll ashore with the financial crisis. How did they fail to foresee the repercussions?

In the heyday of the globalisation consensus, few economists questioned its merits in public. But in 1997, the Harvard economist Dani Rodrik published a slim book that created a stir. Appearing just as the US was about to enter a historic economic boom, Rodrik's book, *Has Globalization Gone Too Far?*, sounded an unusual note of alarm.

Rodrik pointed to a series of dramatic recent events that challenged the idea that growing free trade would be peacefully accepted. In 1995, France had adopted a program of fiscal austerity in order to prepare for entry into the eurozone; trade unions responded with the largest wave of strikes since 1968. In 1996, only five years after the end of the Soviet Union—with Russia's once-protected markets having been forcibly opened, leading to a sudden decline in living standards—a communist won 40% of the vote in Russia's presidential elections. That same year, two years after the passing of the North American Free Trade Agreement

(NAFTA), one of the most ambitious multinational deals ever accomplished, a white nationalist running on an "America first" program of economic protectionism did surprisingly well in the presidential primaries of the Republican party.

What was the pathology of which all of these disturbing events were symptoms? For Rodrik, it was "the process that has come to be called 'globalisation.'" Since the 1980s, and especially following the collapse of the Soviet Union, lowering barriers to international trade had become the axiom of countries everywhere. Tariffs had to be slashed and regulations spiked. Trade unions, which kept wages high and made it harder to fire people, had to be crushed. Governments vied with each other to make their country more hospitable—more "competitive"—for businesses. That meant making labour cheaper and regulations looser, often in countries that had once tried their hand at socialism, or had spent years protecting "homegrown" industries with tariffs.

These moves were generally applauded by economists. After all, their profession had long embraced the principle of comparative advantage—simply put, the idea countries will trade with each other in order to gain what each lacks, thereby benefiting both. In theory, then, the globalisation of trade in goods and services would benefit consumers in rich countries by giving them access to inexpensive goods produced by cheaper labour in poorer countries, and this demand, in turn, would help grow the economies of those poorer countries.

But the social cost, in Rodrik's dissenting view, was high—and consistently underestimated by economists. He noted that since the 1970s, lower-skilled European and American workers had endured a major fall in the real value of their wages, which dropped by more than 20%. Workers were suffering more spells of unemployment, more volatility in the hours they were expected to work.

While many economists attributed much of the insecurity to technological change—sophisticated new machines displacing low-skilled workers—Rodrik suggested that the process of globalisation should shoulder more of the blame. It was, in particular, the competition between workers in developing and developed countries that helped drive down wages and job security for workers in developed countries. Over and over, they would be held hostage to the possibility that their business would up and leave, in order to find cheap labour in other parts of the world; they had to accept restraints on their salaries—or else. Opinion polls registered their strong levels of anxiety and insecurity, and the political effects were becoming more visible. Rodrik foresaw that the cost of greater "economic integration" would be greater "social disintegration". The inevitable result would be a huge political backlash.

As Rodrik would later recall, other economists tended to dismiss his arguments—or fear them. Paul Krugman, who would win the Nobel prize in 2008 for his earlier work in trade theory and economic geography, privately warned Rodrik that his work would give "ammunition to the barbarians."

It was a tacit acknowledgment that pro-globalisation economists, journalists and politicians had come under growing pressure from a new movement on the left, who were raising concerns very similar to Rodrik's. Over the course of the 1990s, an unwieldy international coalition had begun to contest the notion that globalisation was good. Called "anti-globalisation" by the media, and the "alter-globalisation" or "global justice" movement by its participants, it tried to draw attention to the devastating effect that free trade policies were having, especially in the developing world, where globalisation was supposed to be having its most beneficial effect. This was a time when figures such as the *New York Times* columnist Thomas Friedman had given the topic a glitzy prominence by documenting his time among what he gratingly called "globalutionaries:" chatting amiably with the CEO of Monsanto one day, gawking at lingerie manufacturers in Sri Lanka the next. Activists were intent on showing a much darker picture, revealing how the record of globalisation consisted mostly of farmers pushed off their land and the rampant proliferation of sweatshops. They also implicated the highest world bodies in their critique: the G7, World Bank and IMF. In 1999, the movement reached a high point when a unique coalition of trade unions and environmentalists managed to shut down the meeting of the World Trade Organization in Seattle.

In a state of panic, economists responded with a flood of columns and books that defended the necessity of a more open global market economy, in tones ranging from grandiose to sarcastic. In January 2000, Krugman used his first piece as a New York Times columnist to denounce the "trashing" of the WTO, calling it "a sad irony that the cause that has finally awakened the long-dormant American left is that of—yes!—denying opportunity to third-world workers."

Where Krugman was derisive, others were solemn, putting the contemporary fight against the "anti-globalisation" left in a continuum of struggles for liberty. "Liberals, social democrats and moderate conservatives are on the same side in the great battles against religious fanatics, obscurantists, extreme environmentalists, fascists, Marxists and, of course, contemporary anti-globalisers," wrote the *Financial Times* columnist and former World Bank economist Martin Wolf in his book *Why Globalization Works*. Language like this lent the fight for globalisation the air of an epochal struggle. More common was the rhetoric of figures such as Friedman, who in his book *The World is Flat* mocked the "pampered American college kids" who, "wearing their branded clothing, began to get interested in sweatshops as a way of expiating their guilt."

Arguments against the global justice movement rested on the idea that the ultimate benefits of a more open and integrated economy would outweigh the downsides. "Freer trade is associated with higher growth and ... higher growth is associated with reduced poverty," wrote the Columbia University economist Jagdish Bhagwati in his book *In Defense of Globalization*. "Hence, growth reduces poverty." No matter how troubling some of the local effects, the implication went, globalisation promised a greater good.

The fact that proponents of globalisation now felt compelled to spend much of their time defending it indicates how much visibility the global justice movement had achieved by the early 2000s. Still, over time, the movement lost ground, as a policy consensus settled in favour of globalisation. The proponents of globalisation were determined never to let another gathering be interrupted. They stopped meeting in major cities, and security everywhere was tightened. By the time of the invasion of Iraq, the world's attention had turned from free trade to George Bush and the "war on terror," leaving the globalisation consensus intact.

Above all, there was a widespread perception that globalisation was working as it was supposed to. The local adverse effects that activists pointed to—sweatshop labour, starving farmers—were increasingly obscured by the staggering GDP numbers and fantastical images of gleaming skylines coming out of China. With some lonely exceptions—such as Rodrik and the former World Bank chief and Columbia University professor Joseph Stiglitz—the pursuit of freer trade became a consensus position for economists, commentators and the vast majority of mainstream politicians, to the point where the benefits of free trade seemed to command blind adherence. In a 2006 TV interview, Thomas Friedman was asked whether there was any free trade deal he would not support. He replied that there wasn't, admitting, "I wrote a column supporting the CAFTA, the Caribbean Free Trade initiative. I didn't even know what was in it. I just knew two words: free trade."

In the wake of the financial crisis, the cracks began to show in the consensus on globalisation, to the point that, today, there may no longer be a consensus. Economists who were once ardent proponents of globalisation have become some of its most prominent critics. Erstwhile supporters now concede, at least in part, that it has produced inequality, unemployment and downward pressure on wages. Nuances and criticisms that economists only used to raise in private seminars are finally coming out in the open.

A few months before the financial crisis hit, Krugman was already confessing to a "guilty conscience." In the 1990s, he had been very influential in arguing that global trade with poor countries had only a small effect on workers' wages in rich countries. By 2008, he was having doubts: the data seemed to suggest that the effect was much larger than he had suspected.

In the years that followed, the crash, the crisis of the eurozone and the worldwide drop in the price of oil and other commodities combined to put a huge dent in global trade. Since 2012, the IMF reported in its World Economic Outlook for October 2016, trade was growing at 3% a year—less than half the average of the previous three decades. That month, Martin Wolf argued in a column that globalisation had "lost dynamism," due to a slackening of the world economy, the "exhaustion" of new markets to exploit and a rise in protectionist policies around the world. In an interview earlier this year, Wolf suggested to me that, though he remained convinced globalisation had not been the decisive factor in rising inequality, he had nonetheless not fully foreseen when he was writing *Why Globalization Works* how "radical the implications" of worsening inequality "might be for the US, and therefore the world." Among these implications appears to be a rising distrust of the establishment that is blamed for the inequality. "We have a very big political problem in many of our countries," he said. "The elites—the policymaking business and financial elites—are increasingly disliked. You need to make policy which brings people to think again that their societies are run in a decent and civilised way."

[...]

Over the past year, the opinion pages of prestigious newspapers have been filled with belated, rueful comments from the high priests of globalisation—the men who appeared to have defeated the anti-globalisers two decades earlier. Perhaps the most surprising such transformation has been that of Larry Summers. Possessed of a panoply of elite titles—former chief economist of the World Bank, former Treasury secretary, president emeritus of Harvard, former economic adviser to President Barack Obama—Summers was renowned in the 1990s and 2000s for being a blustery proponent of globalisation. For Summers, it seemed, market logic was so inexorable that its dictates prevailed over every social concern. [...]

Over the last two years, a different, in some ways unrecognizable Larry Summers has been appearing in newspaper editorial pages. More circumspect in tone, this humbler Summers has been arguing that economic opportunities in the developing world are slowing, and that the already rich economies are finding it hard to get out of the crisis. Barring some kind of breakthrough, Summers says, an era of slow growth is here to stay.

In Summers's recent writings, this sombre conclusion has often been paired with a surprising political goal: advocating for a "responsible nationalism." Now he argues that politicians must recognise that "the basic responsibility of government is to maximise the welfare of citizens, not to pursue some abstract concept of the global good."

[...]

Globalization Has Reduced Poverty Around the World

Jan Cienski

Jan Cienski is senior policy editor at Politico Europe *and a former Poland correspondent for the* Economist.

G lobalization is responsible for dramatically reducing the number of abjectly poor people around the world, according to a new study that contradicts the claims of skeptics who say it has worsened global poverty.

"On average economic growth is good for the poor, and trade is good for growth," said the study by the London-based Centre for Economic Policy Research.

The study, prepared for the European Commission by a group of respected economists who surveyed existing literature and studies on globalization, was unambiguous in saying that almost every criticism levelled by free trade's skeptics is wrong.

Many globalization critics are "poorly informed about the historical record, and appear not to be aware of the contribution played by globalization in the struggle against poverty," the study's authors say.

They say closer economic ties between countries, reduced tariffs and greater flows of investments have made the most startling impact on global poverty.

While acknowledging the number of poor people in the world remains "disturbingly high," the study says that in 1950 about 55% of the world's population lived on less than US$1 a day (in constant, inflation-adjusted dollars). By 1992, only 24% of the world's population had to make do with that tiny amount. During that time the number of poor remained static at about 1.3 billion people, while the global population grew rapidly.

"Globalization Cures Poverty: Study," by Jan Cienski, Global Policy Forum. Reprinted by permission.

"The proportion of the world's population living in absolute poverty is lower now than it has ever been," the report says.

The study echoes a recent World Bank report which found the degree of an economy's openness is closely linked to its standard of living.

The support for the often-controversial position of continuing to lower tariffs and expand free trade was a little much for the European Commission, which represents governments of various stripes and stressed that the study was not its official position.

"In many respects, the findings will prove controversial, at least to those outside the circle of professional economists, contradicting as they do certain deeply held beliefs about the negative consequences of globalization," wrote Romano Prodi, the European Commission President.

The study notes that, while there are fewer people in abject poverty, the gap between average incomes in rich and poor countries is wider.

Improved communications has had the perverse effect of undermining the case for globalization because "the poor that remain, though a shrinking proportion of the whole population, are more than ever aware of their relative deprivation."

Technology also makes it easier to draw attention to the startling discrepancies in world incomes.

The study takes issue with the slogans of protesters at anti-globalization rallies, like the one in Calgary during last month's G8 summit at Kananaskis, Alta.

Critics charge globalization with increasing inequality, polluting the environment, exploiting workers, undermining the ability of governments to raise taxes to provide health care and welfare and with causing economic instability.

Untrue, according to the study.

"Many of the charges against globalization are misguided," says the study, which says that while globalization does carry some costs, they are more than outweighed by the benefits.

The drumbeat of protest about manufacturers such as Nike and the Gap using Third World sweatshops to make their products actually harms the workers in those factories.

While a salary of $5 a day may seem "shockingly poor" to protesters in rich countries, that is often five times more than the workers would have gotten by staying in traditional industries such as agriculture, the study says.

Although there is some proof that countries exporting energy and natural resources such as timber underprice those products, causing environmental harm, there is no evidence of a "race to the bottom" in wages or environmental standards.

Many critics contend that corporations will relentlessly hunt for the cheapest place to do business, forcing richer countries to gut their social safety nets and environmental rules to match those of the lowest-cost country.

"If low wages alone were enough of an attraction, more [investment] would have flowed to the poorest countries in Africa, rather than predominantly to a small number of middle-income countries in Asia and Latin America," it says.

In fact, it is in Africa that the study finds the weakest international performers, and failed economies that drag down the statistics for the rest of the world.

Recognizing that skeptics often make a better case than the proponents of deeper globalization, the study recommends that rich countries do a better job of explaining the benefits of globalization or else risk a backlash similar to the one that ended the last burst of freer trade that lasted from 1870 to 1913.

The study also recommended the wealthiest nations commit to lowering tariffs and subsidies for agriculture and textiles, which would boost incomes of the poorest workers and farmers, and also increase their foreign aid to 0.7% of GDP.

Currently, only Scandinavians, Luxembourg and the Netherlands give that much. Canada gives only 0.24% of GDP in aid, while the United States gives only 0.1% of GDP.

The study's optimistic conclusions were discounted by globalization skeptics, who saw it as one of a host of biased reports aimed at confirming the reigning orthodoxy.

"For the last 25 years, globalization has been heavily tilted in favour of banks and investors and against the interests of working people," said Robert Scott, an economist at the Economic Policy Institute, a left-leaning Washington-based think-tank.

He charged that the numbers showing poverty reduction were skewed by the exceptional cases of China and India. Removing those two huge nations creates a much more ambiguous case for globalization and shows dramatic increases in global inequality, Dr. Scott said.

"The evidence shows that unregulated capital and trade flows contribute to rising inequality and impede progress in poverty reduction," a new Economic Policy Institute study said."

With Proper Steps, the Poor Can Benefit from Globalization

Matt Nesvisky

Matt Nesvisky has written for the National Bureau of Economic Research, a private nonprofit organization founded in 1920 and dedicated to economic research.

> *"The evidence strongly suggests that export growth and incoming foreign investment have reduced poverty everywhere from Mexico to India to Poland. Yet at the same time currency crises can cripple the poor."*

Does globalization, as its advocates maintain, help spread the wealth? Or, as its critics charge, does globalization hurt the poor? In a new book titled *Globalization and Poverty*, edited by NBER Research Associate Ann Harrison, 15 economists consider these and other questions. In Globalization and Poverty (NBER Working Paper No. 12347), Harrison summarizes many of the findings in the book. Her central conclusion is that the poor will indeed benefit from globalization if the appropriate complementary policies and institutions are in place.

Harrison first notes that most of the evidence on the links between globalization and poverty is indirect. To be sure, as developing countries have become increasingly integrated into the world trading system over the past 20 years, world poverty rates have steadily fallen. Yet little evidence exists to show a clear-cut cause-and-effect relationship between these two phenomena.

Many of the studies in *Globalization and Poverty* in fact suggest that globalization has been associated with rising inequality, and that the poor do not always share in the gains from trade. Other themes emerge from the book. One is that the poor in countries with an abundance of unskilled labor do not always gain from trade

"Globalization and Poverty," by Matt Nesvisky, National Bureau of Economic Research, April 12, 2018, http://www.nber.org/digest/mar07/w12347.html.

reform. Another is that the poor are more likely to share in the gains from globalization when workers enjoy maximum mobility, especially from contracting economic sectors into expanding sectors (India and Colombia). Gains likewise arise when poor farmers have access to credit and technical know-how (Zambia), when poor farmers have such social safety nets as income support (Mexico) and when food aid is well targeted (Ethiopia).

The evidence strongly suggests that export growth and incoming foreign investment have reduced poverty everywhere from Mexico to India to Poland. Yet at the same time currency crises can cripple the poor. In Indonesia, poverty rates increased by at least 50 percent after the 1997 currency crisis in that country, and the poor in Mexico have yet to recover from the pummeling of the peso in 1995.

Without doubt, Harrison asserts, globalization produces both winners and losers among the poor. In Mexico, for example, small and medium corn growers saw their incomes halved in the 1990s, while larger corn growers prospered. In other countries, poor workers in exporting sectors or in sectors with foreign investment gained from trade and investment reforms, while poverty rates increased in previously protected areas that were exposed to import competition. Even within a country, a trade reform may hurt rural agricultural producers and benefit rural or urban consumers of those farmers' products.

The relationship between globalization and poverty is complex, Harrison acknowledges, yet she says that a number of persuasive conclusions may be drawn from the studies in *Globalization and Poverty*. One conclusion is that the relationship depends not just on trade or financial globalization but on the interaction of globalization with the rest of the economic environment: investments in human capital and infrastructure, promotion of credit and technical assistance to farmers, worthy institutions and governance, and macroeconomic stability, including flexible exchange rates. The existence of such conditions, Harrison writes, is emerging as a critical theme for multilateral institutions like the World Bank.

Harrison adds that more research is needed to identify whether labor legislation protects only the rights of those few workers who typically account for the formal sector in developing economies, or whether such legislation softens short-term adjustment costs and helps the labor force benefit from globalization. Anti-sweatshop activism suggests that selective interventions may be successful in this regard.

Harrison next notes that while many economists predicted that developing countries with great numbers of unskilled workers would benefit from globalization through increased demand for their unskilled-intensive goods, this view is too simple and often inconsistent with the facts. Cross-country studies document that globalization has been accompanied by increasing inequality within developing countries, suggesting an offset of some of the reductions in poverty.

Globalization and Poverty yields several implications. First, impediments to exports from developing countries worsen poverty in those countries. Second, careful targeting is necessary to address the poor in different countries who are likely to be hurt by globalization. Finally, the evidence suggests that relying on trade or foreign investment alone is not enough to alleviate poverty. The poor need education, improved infrastructure, access to credit and the ability to relocate out of contracting sectors into expanding ones to take advantage of trade reforms.

Free Trade Fosters Economic Development in Poor Countries

Daniella Markheim

Daniella Markheim is a former senior analyst on trade policy for the Heritage Foundation, a conservative American think tank based in Washington, DC.

U S trade policy and the impact of globalization on America are regularly the subjects of contentious debate both on Capitol Hill and in the media, and 2007 promises more of the same. The free trade argument is played out between those that fear the perceived negative effects of freer trade on their own narrow interests and those that embrace the economic and strategic benefits that open market policies will bring to the economy as a whole. Consequently, in today's policy world, free trade legislation passes on the margin, where every vote is critical. The loss of even a few proponents of freer Trade policies could result in a costly shift away from the open market policies that have helped to bolster America's economic growth.

With free trade agreements (FTAs) with Peru, Colombia, Panama, and South Korea needing congressional approval; Trade Adjustment Assistance up for renewal; the struggle to advance multilateral Trade talks in the World Trade Organization (WTO); and, critically, the need to extend the President's trade promotion authority (TPA) this summer, policymakers have ample opportunity to implement a more protectionist policy stance or to stay the course and continue to allow America to reap the benefits of open market policies.

Hiding from or ignoring the debate about globalization and its effect on the US will not promote a free trade agenda. Rather, this approach merely leaves the voice of protectionism as the

"Why Free Trade Works for America," by Daniella Markheim, The Heritage Foundation, April 16, 2007. Reprinted by permission.

only voice heard on trade policy issues. Instead, a firm public commitment to advancing sound open market policies coupled with a presentation of the facts about the effect of freer trade and investment on America will better help to advance the cause of open market policies. For America to continue to reap the benefits of globalization and to lead the world in demonstrating how globalization progresses and evolves, the President and Congress should make a solid and public commitment to advancing open market policies.

Without political leadership on trade issues, the facts behind the benefits of America's international trade and investment policies will have to suffice in the battle to keep US markets open and global trade liberalization moving forward. Not only does trade liberalization make sense from a theoretical perspective, but the data show that freer trade promotes economic growth and prosperity.

Free trade is about beating poverty and expanding economic opportunity-markedly nonpartisan issues. While working through trade policy legislation this year, Congress will have the opportunity to advocate free trade and to help America and the world reap the rewards that accrue from such policies. It is essential that lawmakers separate myth from fact and assess upcoming trade initiatives objectively. Armed with the facts, they can then help to ensure that prosperity in the US and around the world has a real chance to thrive, both this year and in the longer term.

The Tangible Benefits of Trade

The gains from freer trade are substantial. Today, the $12 trillion US economy is bolstered by free trade, a pillar of America's vitality. In 2005, US exports to the rest of the world totaled $1.2 trillion and supported one in five US manufacturing jobs. jobs directly linked to the export of goods pay 13 percent to 18 percent more than other US jobs.[1] Moreover, agricultural exports hit a record high in 2005 and now account for 926,000 jobs.[2]

In Colorado, international trade supports one of every 20 private-sector jobs and more than 16 percent of manufacturing jobs. International trade supports an estimated 6.1 percent of Ohio's total private-sector employment and more than 20 percent of all manufacturing jobs. In South Carolina, trade supports one of every 10 private-sector jobs and more than 23 percent of manufacturing jobs.[3] State by state across America, international trade promotes opportunity.

The service sector accounts for roughly 79 percent of the US economy and 30 percent of the value of American exports.[4] Service industries account for eight out of every 10 jobs in the US and provide more jobs than the rest of the economy combined. Over the past 20 years, service industries have contributed about 40 million new jobs across America.[5]

As today's global economy offers unparalleled opportunities for the US, continuing to expand trade by lowering barriers to goods and services is in America's economic interest. Freer trade policies have created a level of competition in today's open market that engenders innovation and leads to better products, higher-paying jobs, new markets, and increased savings and investment. Small business, a critical component of the US economy, creates two out of every three new jobs and accounts for about one-quarter of America's exports.[6]

With more than 95 percent of the world's consumers living outside of the United States, the global marketplace is important to US firms. Free trade opens the door to that marketplace and promotes America's continuing prosperity.

For over five decades, the US has earned benefits from reducing its trade barriers, paving the way for substantial economic expansion and higher standards of living. Some specific facts about free trade and the US economy:

- The average US tariff rate on all goods has fallen from over 19 percent in 1933 to 1.8 percent in 2004.
- As a percentage of GDP, the importance of trade in the economy has climbed from single digits in the 1930s to nearly one-quarter of US GDP in 2004.

- At the same time that trade has become freer, real per capita GDP in the US (in constant 2000 dollars) has climbed from a low of $5,061 in 1933 to about $36,000 in 2004.

Freer trade has been a driving force behind America's high standard of living and promises even more if trade barriers can be broken down even further. The Institute for International Economics estimates that over the past 50 years, trade liberalization has brought an additional $9,000 per year to the typical American household.[7] The North American Free Trade Agreement (NAFTA) and the Uruguay Round of the WTO-the two major agreements of the 1990s-generate annual benefits of $1,300-$2,000 for the average American family of four.[8]

Freer trade enables more goods and services to reach American consumers at lower prices, giving families more income to save or spend on other goods and services. Moreover, the benefits of free trade extend well beyond American households. Free trade helps to spread freedom globally, reinforces the rule of law, and fosters economic development in poor countries. The World Bank reports that in the 1990s, per capita real income grew three times faster in developing countries that lowered Trade barriers than in developing countries that did not do so. In fact, over the past 25 years, roughly 500 million people have been lifted from poverty largely as a result of freer trade and market reforms.[9]

US Free Trade Agreements

With 150 members in the WTO, the United States benefits from the increased market access generated by past multilateral agreements. Along with multilateral trade liberalization in the WTO, regional and bilateral free trade agreements also serve as important US trade policy tools.[10] The US has been seeking comprehensive and high-standard trade agreements that are "tailored to reflect a world of high technology, complex new intellectual property standards, labor and environmental considerations, and the growth of the service sector."[11]

While multilateral negotiations take time, FTAs allow the US to make agreements with countries that are willing to dismantle foreign trade barriers rapidly. In the process, FTAs formed with different countries or regions can serve as building blocks for broader agreements and provide institutional competition that helps to keep multilateral talks on track.

As of April 2007, the US has 10 FTAs with 16 countries: Israel; Canada and Mexico (NAFTA); Jordan; Singapore; Chile; Australia; Bahrain; Oman; Morocco; and the Dominican Republic, Costa Rica, El Salvador, Guatemala, Honduras, and Nicaragua (DR-CAFTA).[12]

While some countries are still working to implement more recent trade agreement legislation, the US has already seen impressive results. The FTAs account for more than $900 billion in two-way trade, which is about 36 percent of the total of US trade with the world. US exports to FTA partner countries are growing twice as fast as US exports to countries that do not share FTAs with the US.[13]

The oft-demonized NAFTA has in fact generated significant gains for the US since its inception. Canada and Mexico are America's first and second largest Trade partners, accounting for about 36 percent of all US export growth in 2005.[14] Between 1993 and 2005, US manufacturing and agriculture exports to Canada and Mexico grew by 133 percent and 55 percent, respectively. Each day, NAFTA countries conduct roughly $2.2 billion in trilateral trade.[15] This trade supports US jobs, bolsters productivity, and promotes investment.

Whether the US pursues freer trade through multilateral negotiations or through bilateral agreements, the result is fair and beneficial for America. Similar to the objectives sought by US negotiators in the WTO, US free trade agreements go beyond winning lower tariffs on American agriculture, manufacturing, and services exports. FTAs include provisions that safeguard investors from discrimination, increase regulatory transparency, protect and enforce intellectual property rights, combat corruptive practices, protect and strengthen labor rights, and support environmental protection. The US Trade Representative (USTR) negotiates agreements that include transparent dispute resolution and arbitration mechanisms to guarantee that the agreements are upheld along with the rights of US firms and consumers.

Each element of an FTA strengthens the transparent and efficient flow of goods, services, and investments between member countries. Both FTAs and multilateral trade liberalization open markets, protect investors, and increase economic opportunity and prosperity. In short, freer trade policies serve to promote US interests, not to weaken them or to place an unfair burden on Americans.

Free Trade Is Fair Trade

An artificial distinction has been drawn between "free trade" and "fair trade." The idea that free trade is fair only if countries share identical labor costs and economic regulations or if domestic producers are compensated for market losses to more competitive foreign producers is false. The economic benefits of free trade derive partly from the fact that trading partners are different, allowing any country embracing world markets a chance to be competitive. Free trade is fair when countries with different advantages are allowed to trade with a minimum of restriction and capitalize on those differences.

Low wage costs, access to cheap capital, education levels, and other fundamental variables all play a role in determining the comparative advantages that one country has over another in the global marketplace. To "fairly" equalize those differences-provided those differences are based on a country's economic and demographic reality-only negates or reduces a country's ability to benefit from participating in the global trade system.

Such "fairness" also prevents countries from realizing the tangible gains from freer trade: a more competitive economic environment and better, more efficient domestic resource allocation. These positive effects drive greater long-term economic potential, create economic opportunity, better promote a cleaner environment, and improve living standards at home.

Free trade allows a county to compete in the global market according to its fundamental economic strengths and to reap the productivity and efficiency gains that promote long-run wealth and prosperity. In reality, there is no distinction between free trade and truly fair trade.

[…]

References

1 Office of the US Trade Representative, *2006 Trade Policy Agenda and 2005 Annual Report,* March 2006, at *www.ustr.gov/assets/ Document_Library/Reports_ Publications/2006/2006_Trade_Policy_Agenda/asset_upload_file765_9077.pdf* (January 24, 2007).

2 *Ibid.*

3 US Department of Commerce, International Trade Administration, "Exports, Jobs, and Foreign Investment," at *http://ita.doc.gov/td/industry/otea/state_reports* (April 1, 2007).

4 US Department of Commerce, Bureau of Economic Analysis, "International Economic Accounts," at *www.bea.gov/International/Index.htm* (January 24, 2007).

5 Office of the US Trade Representative, "Free Trade in Services: Opening Dynamic New Markets, Supporting Good Jobs," May 31, 2005, at *www.ustr.gov/Document_ Library/Fact_Sheets/2005/ Free_Trade_in_Services_Opening_Dynamic_New_ Markets,_Supporting_Good_Jobs.html* (March 30, 2007).

6 George W. Bush, "President Bush Addresses Small Business Week Conference," The White House, Office of the Press Secretary, April 13, 2006, at *www.whitehouse.gov/ news/releases/2006/04/20060413-2.html* (March 30, 2007).

7 C. Fred Bergsten, "A New Foreign Economic Policy for the United States," in C. Fred Bergsten, ed., *The United States and the World Economy* (Washington, D.C.: Institute for International Economics, 2005), at *www.iie.com/publications/ chapters_preview/3802/1iie3802.pdf* (March 30, 2007).

8 Office of the US Trade Representative, "Trade Delivers Growth, Jobs, Prosperity and Security at Home," July 2006, at *www.fas.usda.gov/itp/Policy/2006- 07factsheettradedelivers2.pdf* (January 24, 2007).

9 Paul Wolfowitz, "The Challenges of Global Development," speech before the Frankfurt, Germany, Chamber of Commerce and Industry, May 31, 2006, at *http:// go.worldbank.org/DLWIJNDAK0* (March 30, 2007).

10 Based on the strategy of "competitive liberalization," the Bush Administration has been working to advance free and open trade simultaneously on all fronts: bilateral, regional, and multilateral.

11 Office of the US Trade Representative, *2006 Trade Policy Agenda and 2005 Annual Report*, p. 3.

12 Dominican Republic-Central America Free Trade Agreement.

13 Office of the US Trade Representative, *2006 Trade Policy Agenda and 2005 Annual Report*, p. 3.

14 US Department of Commerce, "International Economic Accounts."

15 Office of the US Trade Representative, "NAFTA: A Strong Record of Success," March 2006, at *www.ustr.gov/assets/ Document_Library/Fact_Sheets/2006/asset_ upload_file242_9156.pdf* (January 24, 2007).

Organizations to Contact

The editors have compiled the following list of organizations concerned with the issues debated in this book. The descriptions are derived from materials provided by the organizations. All have publications or information available for interested readers. This list was compiled on the date of publication of the present volume; the information provided here may change. Be aware that many organizations take several weeks or longer to respond to inquiries, so allow as much time as possible.

American Economic Association (AEA)
2014 Broadway Suite 305
Nashville, TN 37203
phone: (615) 322-2595
website: www.aeaweb.org

The American Economic Association (AEA) is a nonprofit, nonpartisan scholarly association dedicated to the discussion and publication of economic research. With career-enhancing programs and services, the AEA works to support both established and prospective economists.

American Institute for Economic Research (AEIR)
phone: (888) 528-1216
email: info@aier.org
website: www.aier.org

Founded in 1933, the American Institute for Economic Research (AIER) works to educate Americans on the value of personal freedom, free enterprise, property rights, limited government, and sound money. The AIER's scientific research shows the importance of these principles in advancing human peace, prosperity, and progress.

Cato Institute
1000 Massachusetts Ave, NW
Washington, DC 20001-5403
phone: (202) 842-0200
website: www.cato.org

Founded in 1977, the Cato Institute is a public research organization dedicated to the principles of individual liberty, limited government, free markets, and peace. Working to present citizens with incisive and understandable research, Cato's scholars and analysts conduct independent, nonpartisan research on policy issues.

Center for Financial Stability (CFS)
1120 Avenue of the Americas, 4th Floor
New York, NY 10036
phone: (212) 626-2660
email: info@the-cfs.org
website: www.centerforfinancialstability.org

The Center for Financial Stability (CFS) is an independent, nonprofit, nonpartisan research organization focused on financial markets for the benefit of investors, officials, and the public. The CFS's objectives are to provide high-quality research, build a practitioner-led community, and serve as a private sector check on government activities.

Center for Popular Economics (CPE)
phone: (413) 545-0743
email: info@populareconomics.org
website: www.populareconomics.org

Founded in 1979, the Center for Popular Economics (CPE) is a nonprofit collective of political economist based in Amherst, Massachusetts. CPE examines the root causes of economic inequality and injustice, and provides a forum for activists, organizers, educators, and progressive economists to come together.

CorpWatch
1958 University Avenue
Berkeley, CA 94704
phone: (341) 359-5760
email: pratap@corpwatch.org
website: www.corpwatch.org

CorpWatch seeks to promote environmental, social, and human rights at the local, national, and global levels by holding multinational corporations accountable for their actions. Utilizing investigative research and journalism to provide important information on corporate corruption and profiteering, CorpWatch works to create a more informed public and effective democracy.

European Free Trade Association (EFTA)
email: mail.gva@efta.int
website: www.efta.int

The European Free Trade Association is an intergovernmental organization created to promote free trade and economic integration for the benefit of its four members—Iceland, Liechtenstein, Norway, and Switzerland—and their trading partners around the world.

Global Policy Forum
205 E. 42nd St., 20th Floor
New York, NY 10017
email: gpf@globalpolicy.org
website: www.globalpolicy.org

Global Policy Forum is an independent watchdog group that tracks the work of the United Nations and scrutinizes global policymaking. They promote accountability and the participation of citizens in decisions about peace and security, social justice, and international law.

Institute of Economic Growth (IEG)
email: system@iegindia.org
website: www.iegindia.org

The Institute of Economic Growth (IEG) is an autonomous multidisciplinary center for advanced research and training in the fields of economics and social development. Established in 1958, the IEG's economists, demographers, and sociologists focus on emerging cutting-edge areas of social and policy concern.

International Chamber of Commerce (ICC)
email: icc@iccwbo.org
website: www.iccwbo.org

The International Chamber of Commerce (ICC) is the world's largest business organization that helps businesses of all sizes and in all countries to operate globally and responsibly. The ICC works to promote international trade, responsible business conduct, and a global approach to regulation that accelerates inclusive and sustainable growth for the benefit of all.

International Forum on Globalization (IFG)
1009 General Kennedy Avenue #2
San Francisco, CA 94129, USA
phone: (415) 561-7650
email: ifg@ifg.org
website: www.ifg.org

The International Forum on Globalization (IFG) is a research and educational institution comprised of leading activists, economists, scholars, and researchers who provide analysis and critique on the cultural, social, political, and environmental impacts of economic globalization.

International NGO Training and Research Centre (INTRAC)
email: info@intrac.org
website: www.intrac.org

Founded in 1991, the International NGO Training and Research Centre (INTRAC) is a nonprofit organization and independent charity that works to strengthen the effectiveness of civil society to combat poverty and inequality, empowering people to gain greater control of their lives.

National Bureau of Economic Research
1050 Massachusetts Ave.
Cambridge, MA 02138
phone: (617) 868-3900
email: info@nber.org
website: www.nber.org

The National Bureau of Economic Research is a private nonprofit, nonpartisan organization founded in 1920. It is dedicated to carrying out economic research and to spreading research findings to academics, public policy makers, and business professionals.

Western Economic Association International (WEAI)
18837 Brookhurst Street, Suite 304
Fountain Valley, CA 92708-7302
phone: (714) 965-8800
website: www.weai.org

The Western Economic Association International (WEAI) is a nonprofit educational organization dedicated to encouraging and communicating economic research and analysis. Founded in 1922, the WEAI's main activities include publishing two quarterly journals and staging forums for current economic research through scholarly conferences.

World Trade Organization (WTO)
email: enquiries@wto.org
website: www.wto.org

The World Trade Organization (WTO) is an international governmental organization that regulates trade between nations. A large majority of the world's trading nations have negotiated, signed, and ratified the WTO's agreements, laying the legal ground rules for international commerce.

Bibliography

Books

David Andrews. *Business Without Borders: Globalization.* Chicago, IL: Heinemann Library, 2011.

John Baylis. *The Globalization of World Politics: An Introduction to International Relations.* Oxford, UK: Oxford University Press, 2017.

Ian Bremmer. *Us vs. Them: The Failure of Globalism.* New York, NY: Penguin Books, 2018.

Joann Chirico. *Globalization: Prospects and Problems.* Thousand Oaks, CA: SAGE Publications, 2013.

Thomas Hylland Eriksen. *Globalization: The Key Concepts.* London, UK: Bloomsbury, 2014.

James D. Gwartney et al. *Common Sense Economics: What Everyone Should Know About Wealth and Prosperity.* New York, NY: St. Martin's Press, 2016.

Elisabeth Hershbach. *Global Inequalities and the Fair Trade Movement.* Philadelphia, PA: Mason Crest, 2017.

Jason Hickel. *The Divide: A Brief Guide to Global Inequality and Its Solutions.* London, UK: Random House Group, 2017.

Donald Jeffries. *Survival of the Richest: How the Corruption of the Marketplace Created the Greatest Conspiracy of All.* New York, NY: Skyhorse Publishing, 2017.

Robert Kuttner. *Can Democracy Survive Global Capitalism?* New York, NY: W.W. Norton & Company, 2018.

Branko Milanovic. *Global Inequality: A New Approach for the Age of Globalization.* Cambridge, MA: Harvard University Press, 2018.

Sheila Nelson. *Cultural Globalization and Celebrating Diversity.* Broomall, PA: Mason Crest Publishers, 2016.

Annelise Orleck. *We Are All Fast-Food Workers Now: The Global Uprising Against Poverty Wages.* Boston, MA: Beacon Press, 2018.

Dani Rodrik. *The Globalization Paradox: Democracy and the Future of the World Economy.* New York, NY: W.W. Norton & Company, 2012.

Manfred B. Steger. *Globalization: A Very Short Introduction.* Oxford, UK: Oxford University Press, 2017.

Joseph E. Stiglitz. *Globalization and Its Discontents Revisited: Anti-Globalization in the Era of Trump.* New York, NY: W.W. Norton & Company, 2018.

Benjamin C. Waterhouse. *The Land of Enterprise: A Business History of the United States.* New York, NY: Simon & Schuster, 2017.

Periodicals and Internet Sources

Donald J. Boudreaux, "Real Talk on Trade," *US News,* March 20, 2017. https://www.usnews.com/opinion/economic-intelligence/articles/2017-03-20/donald-trump-bernie-sanders-fuel-myth-about-free-trade-and-american-jobs

John Cassidy, "The Good (and Bad) News About Poverty and Global Trade," *New Yorker,* October 6, 2015. https://www.newyorker.com/news/john-cassidy/the-good-and-bad-news-about-poverty-and-global-trade

Lynda Gratton, "The Globalisation of Work—and People," *BBC,* September 7, 2012. https://www.bbc.com/news/business-19476254

Ameenah Gurib-Fakim and Stefan Löfven, "The Future of Work is Coming—and We Need to Find a Global Solution,"

Independent, August 21, 2017. https://www.independent. co.uk/voices/future-of-work-automation-need-to-find-a-global-solution-a7904266.html

Neil Irwin, "Globalization's Backlash Is Here, at Just the Wrong Time," *New York Times,* March 23, 2018. https://www. nytimes.com/2018/03/23/upshot/globalization-pain-and-promise-for-rich-nations.html

Chandran Nair, "If We Want A More Equal World, We Need To Dispel These 5 Economic Myths," *Huffington Post,* July 12, 2017. https://www.huffingtonpost.com/entry/equal-world-myths-economy_us_595fc047e4b0d5b458ea172b

Clyde Prestowitz, "Globalization Doesn't Make as Much Sense as It Used To," *Atlantic,* December 12, 2016. https://www. theatlantic.com/business/archive/2016/12/globalization-trade-history/510380/

Charles Riley, "Modi in Davos: Globalization is Under Attack," *CNN,* January 23, 2018. http://money.cnn.com/2018/01/23/ news/modi-davos-india-globalization/index.html

Jeffrey D. Sachs, "The Shifting Global Landscape," *Boston Globe,* January 22, 2017. https://www.bostonglobe.com/ opinion/2017/01/22/the-shifting-global-landscape/ O844Wwn9EYsB5yXGSVPkLK/story.html

Fareed Zakaria, "Everyone Seems to Agree Globalization Is a Sin. They're Wrong," *Washington Post,* January 19, 2017. https://www.washingtonpost.com/opinions/ everyone-seems-to-agree-globalization-is-a-sin-theyre-wrong/2017/01/19/49bded68-de8b-11e6-918c-99ede3c8cafa_story.html?utm_term=.c9842fc0cbc3

Index

A

Affleck, Ben, 95
Ahiakpor, James C. W., 70–75
Allende, Salvador, 70
Amazon Defense Coalition, 66
Amazon Watch, 66
American Civil War, 47
Amoah, Anthony, 152–160
Appadurai, Arjun, 104–105
Apple Inc., 20, 38
Aristotle, 24
Asian Tigers, 83

B

Bachchan, Amitabh, 95
Balko, Radley, 91–99
Bandow, Doug, 146, 147, 149, 151
Barber, Benjamin, 93
Bardhan, Pranab, 146, 147, 150
Barnett, George A., 95
Bauer, Peter, 97–98
Bentham, Jeremy, 87
Bhagwati, Jagdish, 166
Bill of Rights, 52
birth defects, 65–66
Bradley, Anne, 149
Bretton Woods institutions, 49–51
Brexit, 162

British Broadcasting Company (BBC), 95, 129
British East India Company, 46
Bush, George W., 24, 27–28, 167

C

Cable News Network (CNN), 25, 129
Cabrera, Richard, 65
Café de' Coral, 94
Callejas, Adolfo, 67
Calvin Klein, 91
cancer, 64–66
Caplan, Bryan, 76
Carden, Art, 76–79
Cato Institute, 26
Centre for Economic Policy Research, 170
Chan, Michael, 94
Chevron, 62–69
Chevron Global Issues and Policy, 67
childhood leukemia, 66
Cienski, Jan, 170–173
Clinton, Hillary, 162
Coca-Cola, 91, 103, 127
Columbus, Christopher, 15
Comfort T., Dan-Jumbo, 53–61
Confederation of Indigenous Nationalities of Ecuador (CONAIE), 66

contaminated water, 62–69
Converse, 81, 82
corporate personhood, 48
Cowan, Tyler, 96, 98

D

democratization, 25–26
Dependency Theory, 57–58, 70
Disability Adjusted Life Year (DALY), 40
Disney, 127, 129
Disneyfication, 131
Donzinger, Steven, 67
Duke's Fuqua School of Business, 39
Dutch East India Company, 46

E

Economic Policy Institute, 173
Ecuador's National Cancer Registry, 65
emissions, 40–41
Emmanuel, Arghiri, 58–59
Engels, Friedrich, 118
Etim, Akpan Ekom, 53–61
European Commission, 170–173

F

Facebook, 134–142
factor endowment, 152, 155
Fifth Amendment, 49
First Amendment, 49

Fourteenth Amendment, 48
Freedom House, 25–26
free trade, 152–160, 177–184
free trade agreements (FTAs), 50, 163, 177, 180–182
Freund, Charles Paul, 95
Friedman, Thomas, 165, 166, 167

G

Ganguly, Meenakshi, 88
Gap, the, 81, 91, 172
Garrigo, Silvia, 67
Gates, Bill, 129
gender reform, 136
General Agreement on Tariffs and Trade (GATT), 30, 49–51, 154, 156
George, Henry, 153
Gifford, Kathie Lee, 82
Goethe, Johann Wolfgang von, 118
Great Depression, 30, 38
Griswold, Daniel, 24–28
gross domestic product (GDP), 16, 21, 45, 156, 157, 167, 172, 179–180
gross national income (GNI), 154

H

Hall, Stuart, 100, 104
Hanlon, Seth, 39